High Praise for *RKBA*!

"It is said that gun control and abortion are the two most polarized ideological disputes in the US. Perhaps you're against guns, or perhaps like me you've carried one as a cop and/or an armed citizen your entire adult life. Either way, you'll understand some of what drives this complex debate after reading Skip Coryell's essay collection, "RKBA."

– Massad Ayoob
Founder, Lethal Force Institute
Author of "In the Gravest Extreme" – "

Skip Coryell's new book 'RKBA: Defending the Right to Keep and Bear Arms' should be on the shelf of every American gun owner. Skip's writing style will draw you in, make you feel at ease, and keep you entertained from cover to cover. His years of experience, advocacy and dedication shine through on every page and I especially was impressed with his considerate and thoughtful treatment of open carry which is a topic that is near and dear to me personally."

– John Pierce
Co-founder opencarry.org –

"*RKBA*, from the fertile mind of Skip Coryell is a bold, no nonsense, can't-put-it-down treatise on self defense in America. I've known Skip as a student, an instructor, and as an author and I've never met anyone with a deeper sense of God, Family, and Country. All of this shines through in Skip's latest work. This book is a must read for any serious student of the discipline. Get a copy for yourself and anyone else you care about. "

– Bob Houzenga
Director of Midwest Training Group
Lethal Force Institute Instructor,
6-time National Pistol Champion shooter –

"Skip has hit another one out of the park...Unbridled passion in his work! Incredible research, insight & focus on all that matters... I've spent countless hours with Skip teaching personal defense and know of no one more set on getting straight facts to you! Can't remember the last time I read anything in 2 sittings where it didn't relate to hunting or fishing! Straight forward, easy reading ....wise up America...this is good medicine!"

– Craig Frank
Michigan State Director
Ted Nugent United Sportsmen of America –

More Praise for RKBA

"Insight, experience and passion are not easy to convey...especially via simple black text on a stark white page. Somehow, Skip Coryell manages to crack that code time and again. With his ebullience overpowering and unwavering commitment to 'family' and 'values', the reader slips into the living room of 'life according to Skip' without effort. Thankfully, his is a front door a growing number of readers look forward to passing through..."

– Chuck Perricone
Former Michigan Speaker of the House
Executive Director, MCRGO –

"Skip Coryell is one the most sincere patriots I've had a chance to get to know. Those who love the values this country was founded on, including the right to keep and bear arms, should count themselves blessed to have such a man step forward to defend those values for such a time as this. In an era where leaders are more spineless amoeba than men of conviction, I'm glad to find a kindred spirit who's not afraid to enter the arena wielding his jawbone."

– Steve Deace
WHO Radio AM 1040, Des Moines
Author of "Without a Vision the People Perish"–

"Skip Coryell's RKBA is a fascinating treatise on good versus evil and the practical ways to it. He cites examples and solutions to heartrending situations. He speaks of the freedom of those who take charge of their own destiny and the protection of innocents, and the dark side of doing nothing in the face of evil. This book moves you to look within for answers to questions you don't want to ask ... but must.

– Roger Burdette
IowaCarry Board of Directors –

"In this new book, Skip tackles a number of specific topics, but the consistent theme is self-reliance and common sense. His warrior spirit shines through in each article. The reader is left with plenty of food for thought and some great ammo for conversations with both allies and opponents on this extremely important subject."

– Steve Dulan, MCRGO Attorney
MCRGO Board of Directors –

Skip
Coryell

Author of the Ted Nugent-acclaimed book:
"*Blood in the Streets: Concealed Carry and the OK Corral*"

R
K
B
A

Defending the Right to
Keep and Bear Arms

Published by White Feather Press. (www.whitefeatherpress.com)

ISBN   978-0-9822487-0-6

Printed in the United States of America

Exterior cover photo ©iStockphoto.com/ Stefan Klein

White Feather Press

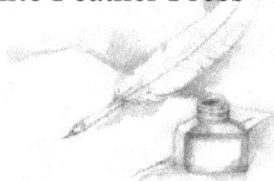

Reaffirming Faith in God, Family, and Country!

Dedication

To my wife, Sara, and all my children.

And to all law-abiding citizens who keep and bear arms
for the protection of others.

Contents

Acknowledgments

I would like to thank the following for their help and encouragement over the years. Without you this book would not have been possible.

Ted, Shemane, and Sasha Nugent and the entire Nugent family.

Craig Frank and the whole tribe of Ted Nugent United Sportsmen of America.

Massad Ayoob and all of Lethal Force Institute for encouragement and top-notch training.

Chuck Perricone, Audrey Perricone, Steve Dulan, Dan Barch, Jim Kleiman and all my friends at Michigan Coalition for Responsible Gun Owners (MCRGO).

Bob Houzenga and Andy Kemp of Midwest Training Group for their excellent instruction.

Dave Stevens, Walt Herwath, Sheriff Dar Leaf and Larry Jackson of Midwest Tactical Training.

Roger Burdette and all my friends at IowaCarry Inc.

And last, but certainly not least, Steve Deace at WHO Radio AM 1040 in Des Moines.

Introduction

Mark Twain, one of my favorite authors, once said:

"In the beginning of a change, the patriot is a scarce man, brave and hated and scorned. When his cause succeeds the timid join him, for then it costs nothing to be a patriot."

I have found this to be very true. Ten percent of the people have, and always will, do ninety percent of the work. It begins when we are still kids on the playground. We try to start up a baseball team only to find that no one wants to be the first to join. Everyone holds back, waiting for the safety of numbers. I suppose that behavior is normal for kids, but the trait disgusts me in adults.

A real patriot doesn't hang back. He leads. Sadly, leaders and patriots are few here in America. This book was written with the recognition that the patriot is indeed a scarce man, brave, and hated and scorned...until he succeeds, then everyone climbs aboard to share in the glory.

My heroes have always been those who lead; those who stand; those who step out from the comfort of the crowd for what they believe in. My hope for you is that you will read this book and become imbued with courage; that you will overcome your fear; that you will follow your convictions and climb aboard. That you may some day lead.

Skip Coryell
The Author

One

America's New Mentality – "Cower and Die"

I'm a stay-at-home dad and the primary caregiver for our 1-year-old son. Even now, as I type this article, there is a 40 caliber semi-automatic pistol on my right hip. I carry a pistol 24/7, 365 days a year. Sometimes it's a nuisance, but I will never kneel at the feet of a madman and whimper while he shoots me and the ones I love. Instead, I will take careful aim, and double-tap the center of exposed mass until the murderer falls to the pavement, no longer a threat to the innocent in society. When faced with a weapon-wielding madman, I don't hide beneath a desk, cowering in the hopes that he'll shoot someone else and then move on. I don't roll the dice and hope for the best. Instead, I take responsibility for my own defense, and I attack. That's what real parents do. They protect those unable to protect themselves, and they do so aggressively and without apology.

Having said all that, I, too, would have been helpless to stop the killing at Virginia Tech, or Columbine, or Pearl, and even at the University of Iowa. What do these places all have in common that render a normally competent, personal protection instructor impotent? They are all pistol-free zones. I like to call them criminal safe zones, where bad guys can feel safe and free to exact all manner of evil upon us, the unarmed public, upon our unarmed defenseless and innocent children. Our government, in its infinite folly, has disarmed us, then broadcast for all criminals to see, exactly when and where they can kill the most unarmed people. It's like a bowling pin shoot: the government lines us up, and the bad guys shoot us down. And when questioned about this insanity, the legislators and other politicians say; "we're doing this for your own good". I haven't heard that since I was a child. But I've got news for you politicians – I'm not a child any longer, and I know what's best for me. When the government starts making laws that preclude me from protecting my one-year-old son, then it's time I campaigned to replace them. Consider yourself forewarned. The people hired you, and the people will fire you.

Yesterday, a crazed, lone, gunman, executed 32 people at the Virginia Tech campus. Today, politicians (our leaders) are calling for more gun control. Call me daft, but I don't get it. Where's the logic? Isn't one definition of insanity "doing the same thing over and over again, but expecting different results?" We've tried gun control. It didn't work. It failed us, and it failed our children. It failed us at the University of Iowa in 1991. It failed us at Columbine High School. It failed us in Pearl, Mississippi, and now, it has failed us again in Blacksburg, Virginia.

Why is everyone on television acting so surprised? This is logic 101. If you disarm everyone except crazed murderers, then only crazed murderers will have guns. Let's face it, most people don't have the expertise or the guts to disarm a gun-wielding madman.

Forgive me for sounding harsh, but gun control is killing us. It's killing innocent children all across our country, and it's been killing them for decades. Why? Because we don't have the guts to stand up to our politically correct legislators and tell them no! Enough is enough! Stop killing our children! All across America, even in states where tens of thousands of people have been trained and licensed to carry a gun for protection, people are hiding under desks, jumping from 2nd floor windows, and cowering beneath the muzzle of a deranged killer. As a general rule, the people who cower in the face of determined evil, are the people who die in a pool of their own blood. It's time America – it's time to fight back!

But do the people of America still have the guts to stand up against elected officials? I honestly don't know. Are we Americans? Are we men and women determined to protect our families, or have we all become sheep, content to follow the shepherd over the precipice to the jagged rocks below? Columbine and Virginia Tech are not good omens. The victims there were unarmed sheep, who hid beneath desks and chairs, simply cowering before they died. They said "Baa" as they were being slaughtered.

Something basic to our society has to change. It's time to stand up and fight while we still have the means to do so. And if our politicians tell us we can't protect our children in a daycare center, or a post office, or a church, then we show them the door. We vote them out. We recall them. We take out the trash. That's the attitude that America was founded on. Somewhere along the timeline, America has lost it's way, we've lost our instinct for survival; it's no longer "fight or flight"; it's just plain "cower and die".

Where did Americans ever get the idea that they could successfully outsource personal protection? I know a guy who won't trust another man to mow his lawn, because only "he" can do it right and to his own satisfaction. But that same particular, finicky person walks around all day long trusting total strangers, who aren't even present, to protect the one thing he cannot replace – his own life.

A word of caution: don't think that the terrorists aren't watching, because they are, and they're taking notes. Once they realize that most Americans are nothing but sheep waiting to be slaughtered, then it's Katie bar the door, because every terrorist and his grandma will be over here killing as many American infidels as they can. America has ceased to be the "land of the free and the home of the brave", and instead has become a target-rich environment, the "ignorant and blissful land of cower and die".

The police cannot protect us; it was never so. The police have their place and their job, but it was never their responsibility to be the bodyguards of every man, woman and child in America. That job is a personal responsibility that most of us have forsaken. It is my job to protect my family; that's why they're called "my" family and not "your" family. I feel silly saying things so basic to life and truth, but, sadly enough, these things need to be said. Trying to outsource personal and family defense will always be a losing proposition.

Take responsibility for protecting yourself and the ones you love. Go ahead and outsource your lawn, but no one can protect your family better than you. It's your job! Do it! Don't give in to the "cower and die" mentality. Instead, crawl out from under that desk and fight for your life. It's a decision you can live with.

The Story Behind the Story

This commentary on the Virginia Tech massacre of April 2007 is probably the one writing that garnered me the most attention for the entire year. I wrote it while living in Iowa far from family and friends.

I remember being furious at America for allowing this to happen. I was so angry that I had to wait a while before I could write it with any clarity and cohesion. Once I'd written it, I sent it off to my friend, Ted Nugent, to get his opinion. He loved it and sent it on to his daughter, Sasha, who immediately published it on tednugent.com. Apparently, there were a lot of people out there who thought like I did. They were sick and tired of letting crazed murderers run rampant all over the country, killing innocents with impunity.

From there, it ended up in the hands of Steve Deace, a popular radio talk show host in Des Moines, Iowa. Steve called and asked me to come on his show. Truth be told, I had never been interviewed in-studio and I was quite nervous. Steve turned out to be a great guy with sharp wit and a keen mind. I remember sitting there with my headphones on waiting for the bumper music to fade away and for Steve to go on the air. He looked over at me and said "Now Skip, I don't want to make you nervous, but as soon as I flip this switch 35,000 people are going to hear your voice." My heart leaped into my throat, but the interview went well and Steve ended up asking me back two times that same year.

You can hear the interview in its entirety by logging on to my website at www.skipcoryell.com. I hope you enjoy the interview and the commentary as well.

Two

Carrying Concealed in the Hawkeye State

For 49 years I've lived in Michigan, hunting its woods, fishing its lakes, and, most importantly, making friends to last a lifetime. I never dreamed of leaving; it wasn't even on the radar screen. But, my wife was offered a great job with a great company, so we packed up last January and moved to Iowa: the land of big bucks, tall corn, and may-issue CCW.

I remember years ago in Michigan, fighting side by side with all of you to get shall-issue passed and its subsequent reforms. It was a long, hard-fought battle, and it still goes on. But the last 9 months in Iowa has been an eye-opener for me. May-issue CCW statutes are a nightmare, and Iowa's statute is the worst kind of nightmare. By law, the County Sheriff has sole discretion over who gets a permit and who does not. He also decides what training, if any, is required, and has freedom to create and abolish pistol-free zones on a whim. There are 99 counties in Iowa, some are close to shall-issue, some issue with severe restrictions, while many don't issue at all. This being the case, I did a lot of research before agreeing to move here. I chose my county wisely, and was issued a nonrestricted CCW permit here in Jones County.

When I moved to Iowa, I thought I'd take a break from political activism: that break lasted about 2 months. By the time the Virginia Tech Massacre happened, I was back into the fight thicker than ever. The week after Virginia Tech, I was interviewed for two hours by Steve Deace on his afternoon drive show in Des Moines. WHO radio, AM 1040, is one of the largest AM talk shows in the Midwest. The topic was my recent article "*Cower and die – the New American Mentality*" and you can listen to the interview in its entirety on my website at www.skipcoryell.com. Steve Deace and I hit it off from the start and I hope to come back to his show this fall to talk about my next book "*Church and State*".

About that time, I was elected to serve on the Board of Directors for the pro-CCW group called IowaCarry, Inc., (www.iowacarry.org) where I now work hard to establish shall-issue CCW in Iowa. But it's going to be a long, hard battle. I'm amazed at the similarities between politicians, regardless of their state of residence. People of power just don't want to give it up, even when it's the right thing to do. They hold on for dear life until it is stripped away from them by dedicated citizens brandishing the power of "We the people" and a never-surrender attitude. Iowa will eventually pass CCW reform, but it may be a slow train coming with many political and public relations hurdles yet to be cleared. But, when it comes right down to it, the people in Iowa aren't much different than Michiganders. They'll fight for the rights that have been stripped from them, and they'll win.

I am very busy here in Iowa. I've just finished the second edition to my pro-CCW book "*Blood in the Streets: Concealed Carry and the OK Corral*". There are two added chapters, along with other updates and added pictures. The book will go on sale on October 1st, 2007. As always, a discount will be offered to MCRGO members. My third novel "*Church and State*" also goes on sale October 1st. "*Church and State*" is a political thriller about the erosion of morality and religious freedom here in America.

On the CCW instruction front, I still return to Michigan once a month to teach Basic CCW classes with my partner, Larry Jackson, in Barry County. We are adding an advanced CCW class in March of 2008. I also teach CCW classes here in Jones County Iowa. In a few days, I'm off to Midwest Training Group to benefit from training with Massad Ayoob's Lethal Force Institute. I'm expecting to learn a lot and have a great time in the process.

Probably the biggest change in my life this year has been the formation of my own publishing company called White Feather Press, LLC. The primary mission of this company is to get books in print which advance the traditional causes of "God, Family, and Country". So to all you closet writers out there, break out your typewriters and give it your best shot. My website www. whitefeatherpress.com will be up and running by December 1st. Submission guidelines must be followed.

So, as you can see, I'm keeping very busy, and while I am happy here in Iowa, I've got to admit that Michigan is a great place to live if you want to carry a concealed pistol for self defense. State

Attorney General, Mike Cox, has done a superb job negotiating reciprocity for Michigan, and your permit is now recognized in 33 states. Contrast that to my Iowa permit, which is good in only 14 states. (A few months ago I took a Utah CCW class just to get my Utah nonresident permit, thereby increasing the states in which I can carry.) Michigan also enjoys the benefits of the recently-passed "Stand your ground" legislation, which was lobbied for and passed in large part due to the unrelenting efforts of MCRGO members. And don't underestimate the importance of Michigan's state preemption law. As you recall, it was MCRGO who led the legal and public relations charge against the cities of Ferndale, Clio, and even my home town of Hastings as they attempted to strip you of your Second Amendment rights one city, town, and village at a time.

I follow and support all the CCW upgrade efforts of MCRGO, and I'm rooting for you as you try to pass legislation ridding the state of those ever-dangerous "criminal safe zones". All of you are blessed to have an organization like MCRGO fighting for you, but don't be caught sitting on the sidelines. If you haven't joined MCRGO, then go to www.mcrgo.org and do so now. The future of Michigan depends on your active role.

See you out in the woods this fall. Happy safe hunting and God bless.

The Story Behind the Story

The above article was written in September of 2007 and then published by Michigan Coalition for Responsible Gun Owners

(MCRGO) the following month. It was designed to read like a "letter to friends back home". I had been living in Iowa for all of 2007 and was missing my friends and family in Michigan. Iowa and the people there were fantastic, but there's just something about the place where you grow up. No matter how far away you move or how long you're gone - home will always be where you spent your childhood.

Iowa was a different experience for me in terms of carrying concealed. Iowa is a may-issue state, but in a very unusual way. Of the 99 Iowa counties, about half of them would issue and the other half would not. So if you lived in the right county, you could get an unrestricted CCW permit.

One of the absolute greatest things about living in Iowa was the bowhunting. I hunted a 500-acre farm across the river from my house. I was used to bowhunting for deer in Michigan where it was very crowded, but there are very few bowhunters in Iowa, comparatively speaking. I recall I went to my neighbor (a corn farmer - go figure) and asked him for permission to hunt his property. He hopped down off his giant tractor, rubbed his wrinkled face for a moment as if I'd just asked him the 10,000-dollar question. Finally he answered "Oh, I suppose ya can. But your going to be out there all by yourself." Inside I was screaming for joy, but outside I simply said "Well, okay. I guess I can still hunt it." We shook hands and it was my best bow season ever. Iowa was a wonderful chapter in my life.

Three

Hell in a Handbasket

I wake up every morning afraid to watch the news. I used to look forward to informing myself, and I always viewed it as a prerequisite to good citizenship. But I'm not so sure I have what it takes to be a good citizen anymore. Sunday morning a police officer murdered 6 teens in Northern Wisconsin. (At the time, my family and I were less than 30 miles away from the murderer.) Less than an hour ago a 14-year old walked into Success Tech High School in Ohio and started shooting. Early reports say he had a gun in each hand and shot 2 teachers and one other student. I watched the news for 15 minutes, but then I had to turn off the television to recover.

It seems to me that the world has gone to hell in a handbasket, running, hurrying, speeding toward destruction. I fear for my children everyday. I wait on the front porch as they get on the bus every morning wondering . . . will they come home tonight? I don't think life was supposed to be like this. How did things get so bad?

Mothers and fathers are drowning their babies, putting them in microwaves, hanging them, shooting them. Husbands and wives are beating each other, dismembering one another, and killing each other with reckless abandon. The world today makes me sick! What happened? How did we get this way? Is there any hope?

And then I open the Bible and it all becomes a little more clear. I read about parents sacrificing their children to the god Molech. I read about brothers selling their siblings into slavery. I read about one race enslaving another. Even the holiest book on the planet is testament to man's brutality. So I'm forced to conclude that we have always been this way. The only difference is the 24-hour news channel brings it all (or most of it) to light for us the moment it happens. We see pictures of human-wrought carnage in our own living rooms, and we sit with our children trying to explain why they need not fear, when, deep down inside, we know there is every reason to fear.

Or, perhaps that's part of the problem. Maybe most of us aren't sitting with our children, eating dinner, watching the carnage, trying to help them process it and make sense of it all. I find it difficult to explain to my 11-year-old son why a classmate would resort to killing his friends - primarily because I don't have the answers. I don't think anyone does.

Nonetheless, I think it's crucial that we talk about it with our kids. The ostrich approach will not work; it never has. Our kids need us to talk about it with them and try to help them make sense of the madness. It's an impossible task, but perhaps if more parents spoke daily to their children, watched them, listened to them, hugged them, corrected them, perhaps, just perhaps, fewer angry, confused 14-year-olds would walk into schools shooting their friends.

My friends on the left say gun control is the answer. I say no. I say child control is the answer. I have noticed that when I don't spend enough time with my children they get into more trouble. But the moment I start to wrestle with them, tickle them, talk to them. They get happy again and their behavior improves. When it comes to children, an ounce of prevention is worth a ton of cure – because there is no cure. Once the shooting starts, it's too late for talking.

In an hour and forty-five minutes my 11-year-old son will get off the bus (I hope) and we'll watch the news together. He will sit there quietly because that's the way he is. But I'll talk to him about the shootings. I'll tell him to run away from the school if it ever happens. If the bad person catches him, I'll instruct him to fight until he escapes. And I'll tell him that sometimes people just go crazy. I'll tell him that some people are evil. And then he'll ask me questions that I can't answer; that in a perfect world he would never even have to ask. But since when have we lived in a perfect world – not since the garden of Eden.

You can talk to your kids until you're blue in the face, but when words fail, when they pale to the task, when evil reaches out and snatches the breath of hope from your lungs, just reach out and hug your children. Press your face to theirs and gently rumple their hair with your hand. Yes, when my son comes home, I'm going to hug him, play with him. And I'll tell him that no matter what else happens in this crazy world, that he can always count on my love. I will always be here for him.

Even if the world goes to hell in a handbasket, tell your kids that you love them, that God loves them, and that these are unwavering constants. There is evil in the world, but there is also good. Teach your children the good in life, because they won't see it on the news.

The Story Behind the Story

This was my second interview of 2007 with Steve Deace at WHO radio AM 1040. As always I found Steve to be an engaging and provocative interviewer. He participates heavily, but without taking control or stifling the guest. On this particular day, we discussed my latest essay titled *"Hell in a Handbasket"*. We spoke about society's downward spiral into graft and corruption, with the root causes being lack of accountability, the systematic and intentional removal of God from all aspects of public society, the breakdown in our criminal justice system, as well as our culture's fascination with destruction and negativity.

Oddly enough, I remember this radio interview most because of the great sacrifice I had to make in order to give it. It was the peak of the rut in Iowa, big buck country, and I couldn't go out hunting that night because of the interview. I recall that I had to go out into my pole barn to get away from the noise of my three children before placing the call. Kids of all ages just don't realize that Dad has important things in his life too. I could be talking to the President of the United States and my daughter would walk up and interrupt me: "Dad! Phillip just told me I was ugly!" And then she would go on and on and on about how terrible he was. I suppose in a way, that's a good thing. I'm approachable.

You can hear the interview in its entirety by logging on to my website at www.skipcoryell.com.

Four

The Best Defense

I remember once, as a boy of 14, I was being bullied at school. I was looking for a way to protect myself. So I asked one of my neighbors, an adult I respected named Cal, this question:

"What is the best form of self defense?"

His answer was immediate and unflinching:

"A kind word."

I was very unhappy with that answer. I had expected him to tell me about some rare form of martial art where high-flying kicks and fists of steel would make me invincible to bullies. Instead, he preached to me about kindness, so I abruptly disregarded his wisdom. Besides, I was already fourteen. What did he know? He was just an adult anyway! Many times since then I have looked back and wished I had taken the man more seriously. It was some of the best advice I've ever ignored.

Since then, I have been in many arguments, fights, altercations, and disagreements. Call them what you want, but none of them were fun and no good ever came from them. In almost every case I should have just walked away.

Now that I carry a pistol, I don't get into fights anymore. I don't argue. I don't gesture disparagingly, and I don't antagonize or challenge unnecessarily. I avoid places where conflict is likely. I avoid crazy people. In my experience, when you let crazy people into your life, your life becomes crazy. I have no use for crazy.

When someone insults me, I try to smile. A smile is confident and disarming. If I can say something witty to diffuse the situation, then I do so. If I can't think of anything good to say, then I keep my mouth shut and walk away.

Ironically, carrying a gun has made me a very polite person.

When I'm insulted, I keep walking. Always keep walking. It may not seem like the most masculine or honorable thing to do, but it is the smartest response. It may save you thousands in legal fees, possible death or injury, and your life will go on undisturbed. If you stop to argue, the situation may escalate, and no good will come of it.

As an NRA Personal Protection Instructor, I get a lot of questions about "What is the best?" People want to know what is the best pistol, the best holster, the best self defense cartridge, etc. I always tell them there is no best for everyone. It's an individual choice that all of us make. We make decisions, and we live with them - or we die with them.

All of us should teach that a firearm is a tool of last resort, which means that there should be many things that occur prior to drawing our pistol in self defense: things like avoidance, retreat, awareness, visualization, range practice, and alertness. These are all good and necessary parts to everyone's personal defense model. But don't underestimate the power of a kind word. It may not always be the best defense, but it is oftentimes the first line of defense.

Now, granted, once the gun is in your face, the time for a kind word has passed. That reminds me of a movie by Patrick Swayze and Sam Elliott called "*Roadhouse*". In the movie, Swayze plays the part of a notorious bar-room "cooler". A cooler is someone who keeps situations from getting out of control by using their experience, their wisdom, and, yes, even kind words. In this particular scene, Swayze is teaching his bouncers the tricks of the trade. It goes something like this:

"If someone gets in your face and calls you a #%$#&^*%# ... be nice. Ask him to walk. Be nice. If he won't walk, walk him. But be nice. If you can't walk him, one of the others will help you, and you'll both, be nice. I want you to be nice, until it's time ... to not be nice."

Now I fully understand that as CPL holders, we're not bouncers. But the principle of kindness and civility is the same. One kind word can diffuse a potential confrontation. A soft smile can allow you to carry on with your life unmolested.

In my classes I teach my students how to make polite eye contact with a passer-by. As someone walks passed, you turn your head slightly in their direction, make momentary eye contact, and give your head a soft nod. When done correctly, you are telling the stranger two things: 1) I'm not afraid of you; I'm not the bottom of the pecking order; don't mess with me. 2) I've gotten a good look at you and I can identify you in a police line-up.

When carrying a pistol, you must consider that every time you interact with another person there is potential for deadly conflict. Let me close by giving you some good advice: Never argue. Never altercate. Never insult.

There is no good that can come from it. Treat everyone you meet with the utmost dignity and respect, and more serious problems can be avoided. As always, the golden rule comes into play: "Do unto others, as you would have others do unto you."

Always practice and stay aware and prepared - just in case you need that tool of last resort. But above all else, always - be nice, until it's time ... to not be nice.

The Story Behind the Story

This article was published by Michigan Coalition for Responsible Gun Owners and also on tednugent.com. It was inspired by one of my childhood heroes. His name is Cal and he lived down the road a piece, walking distance, from my parent's home. To this day he probably has no idea how great an impact he had on my life.

His wife, Jenny, was a college librarian, and Cal was an engineer. They had no children, just two incomes and lots of stuff. I think back then we called them yuppies. I'd never seen a yuppie before. But they were nice people and I liked them from the moment they moved from the city out to the boonies where I lived.

I always looked on them with awe, because they had so much money. We were poor, so Cal got my attention when he drove by pulling their large sailboat to Lake Michigan. Cal was my idol, and I wanted all that money too.

But then something really weird happened. All of a sudden, they both just up and quit their jobs. It was the strangest thing. They started walking around in bib overalls, chewing on grass, moving real slow and just making things they had a mind to.

I remember that in my teenage years, I spent a lot of time down there, mostly doing leatherwork, birdwatching, candle-making, and watching Jenny make quilts. Most weekends they would travel around the state to arts and crafts festivals peddling their wares. Sometimes I would go with them, and I really enjoyed it. But I came to understand very quickly that there was very little money in art, so I shied away from it. I didn't want to be poor like my parents.

Now, 35 years later, I live much the same way that Cal and Jenny did (minus the bib overalls) and I've come to understand and appreciate their decision to leave the rat race behind. In the end, I had to make the same tough decision. I could have kept my corporate job, making a decent wage, buying lots of stuff, living in a big house with two new cars, but, in the end, I decided against the "decent" wage, in lieu of a "decent" life. Of course, either decision would have been okay for me to make, but only one would have made me truly happy.

I learned a lot from Cal. He was a skinny man, a vegetarian who couldn't punch his way out of a wet, paper bag. But he taught me the first and most important rule of self defense. Be nice.

Five

The Power of Control Z

I'm a writer by trade and first and foremost a novelist. I just love a good storyline. A few days ago I was typing away on my laptop, writing a chapter to my latest novel called "*Stalking Natalie*". (It's a good thriller that I believe concealed carry people will love. The main character is a female CPL holder who is being stalked by a serial killer.) I was almost done, having 5 pages written, when my two-year-old son came up and started pressing keys. At the time, I had all 5 pages highlighted and I watched in horror as two hours of irreplaceable work instantly disappeared. My heart rate skyrocketed until I was reminded that all I had to do was press the keys "Control Z" and my pages would magically reappear. Sure enough, I pressed the keys and my chapter came back totally in tact.

And then I got to thinking about it. Wouldn't it be nice if guns came with a Control Z feature? So many innocent lives could be retrieved. Unfortunately though, bullets, much like unkind words, once fired can never be taken back. The damage is done and all of us have to live with the errant decision to pull the trigger at the wrong time. But there's no such thing as "undo" on a gun. It would violate the immutable law of cause and effect. There is no substitute for good judgment.

While I was thinking about it, I was reminded of a family from my childhood. I don't recall their last names, after all, it was 40 years ago. I grew up in rural Michigan during the sixties and early seventies and I remember going to the landfill every week. Back then we just called it "The Dump". My mother would always get mad at my father, because he would take a truckload of trash to drop off, but then search through the rubble for things he liked and bring more trash home. I guess it's true "One man's trash is another man's treasure". Sometimes we would bring our 22 rifles and shoot the rats while old Mac sat up at the front and burned rubber off copper wire for resale. I used to play with Mac's son, who was about my age. They were a black family, the only black family in town, and the only black people I had ever seen, aside from the ones I saw on television. I remember that my dad and old Mac would sit and talk for hours while I played on the trash heaps with his son. My mom got mad about that as well, coming home smelling like garbage with clothes filthy dirty. But I enjoyed our trips to the dump.

Then one day my parents talked at the dinner table about bad people burning crosses in old Mac's back yard. I'd never heard of anything like that and I didn't understand it. People started shooting at Mac's house as well. To a boy in grade school, this was very confusing. I still didn't understand what racism was and wouldn't for many years to come.

Then one day we went to the dump and Old Mac was no longer there. A stranger had taken his place. I asked my father where he went, but he avoided the question. It wasn't until years later that I discovered the full truth.

One day, Old Mac heard a noise in his house during the middle of the night. Because he had been terrorized for so long by racists, he grabbed his shotgun and went to investigate. When he came to the dark kitchen, he saw a man inside, raised his gun and fired. The man slumped to the floor dead. It wasn't until Mac turned on the lights that he realized the full ramifications of his action. There, in a puddle of blood, lay his son.

After that, Mac's wife and children left him, then Mac left as well. It was a sad end to a very tragic story. I always tell my students that we live and die based on the decisions we make. I guess that's true of our loved ones as well. They also can live or die based on the wisdom or folly of our own choices.

I tell this story because almost every month I hear the tragic tale of someone accidentally shooting a person they love. Stories like this continually drive home the importance of the NRA's 4th rule of gun safety: "Know your target and what is beyond."

I'm certain that Old Mac would have sacrificed his own life for the power of "Control Z". But in truth, Control Z doesn't exist, at least not with bullets and guns.

Every last one of us, regardless of our exhaustive training or our spotless records, is capable of making a bad decision that ends with the death of one we love. One second of poor judgment can cause a lifetime of pain. Always be careful. Don't get lax. Always, forever, know your target and what is beyond.

The Story Behind the Story

I grew up in a little hick town in southwest Michigan called Orangeville. Guns were taken for granted there, and I and most of my friends could be seen roving the yards and neighborhoods with BB guns, pellet guns, and even 22 caliber rifles as young as 10 years old. It wasn't a big deal - until someone got shot. But it didn't happen often, hardly at all, actually, and considering the number of guns in our community accidents were really quite rare. But it was always a tragedy when it did occur.

The story below stemmed from an incident that happened during the 1960s when I was quite young. It was during the race riots, Martin Luther King marches, Flower Power and hippies, drugs and free love. But our town was so small that we were fairly insulated from most city problems until years later. My community was rough for a small, rural town, and some would say we were behind the times and even a little backwards in some respects.

I grew up listening to some adults talk of racism, and then watching the race riots from Detroit terrified me as a 10-year boy. But I never feared Old Mac from the county landfill or his young son whom I sometimes played with. They were just people to me and I never questioned the color of their skin.

What happened to Mac and his family was a tragedy. It could have been avoided. Whenever I'm up on the firing line with new shooters and I see them put their finger on the trigger when it shouldn't be, I cringe inside. Bullets, once fired, can never be retrieved, and the damage they do is permanent.

It was a lesson I learned young, as a small boy in a rural town. It was a tragedy that the power of Control Z will never erase.

Six

Gun Control – A Study in Duality

In 1886 one of the greatest authors of the Victorian era, Robert Louis Stevenson, wrote a novella about the duality of man. It soon became a bestseller in both Great Britain and the United States. The story centered around two characters called Dr. Jekyll and Mr. Hyde, who, in reality, turned out to be the same person. It is the classic tale of a split personality.

Here in present-day America, the anti-gunners would have us believe that anyone wishing to carry a firearm also suffers from a split Jekyll-and-Hyde type of personality. In Stevenson's story, the beastly Mr. Hyde is unleashed from within Dr. Jekyll by drinking a potion. Conversely, according to anti-gunners here in America, the evil, dark side of humanity is supposedly unfettered, not by a magic potion, but by the simple presence of an inanimate object called a firearm. Hmmm, could that be true? Are guns magic talisman's of evil (like Frodo's ring) capable of perverting the hearts and minds of the best society has to offer simply by their presence?

There's just one problem with that assertion: it's all fiction. Robert Louis Stevenson got his story line from a dream he had one night. On the other hand, I have no idea why the antis believe that guns are evil tools like magic potions, hell-bent on controlling and consuming us. But one thing is certain, in both cases, with Stevenson's story and with the antis, we are dealing with make-believe, imaginary creatures. Do they also believe in elves? How about aliens from outer space? The Lochness Monster? Maybe Bigfoot is packing heat too and no one has gotten it on film yet? I wonder, does Sasquatch carry a semi-auto or is he a traditional wheelgun man?

In short, for anyone to believe that 174,000 CPL holders here in Michigan have fragile, dual personalities, and are ready to magically transform into raving, violent monsters at the first sign of conflict, just by the mere fact that we carry a firearm for self defense is in itself illogical and patently absurd. According to them, when we are unarmed and defenseless, we are kind, rational and loving members of society (sheep). However, let us strap on a firearm, and the evil Mr. Hyde breaks free from the darkness of our souls to rape, pillage, and plunder the innocents around us!

When someone cuts us off in traffic, the antis are convinced we're going to chase them down and kill them. When our spouse makes us angry by burning dinner, they're afraid we're going to pull our pistol out and shoot them in a fit of rage. There's just one problem with that view of CPL holders: it's not real and it exists only in their own imaginations. By and large, we are all sane, rational, honest, law-abiding citizens who go out of our way to protect and defend our families and friends and neighbors from the worst that society has to offer. And that has been proven over and over again since our CPL law went into effect in 2001. When you look at the facts, we're just not that scary.

I submit to you that the opposite is true: we're not the scary ones – they are. After all, they are the ones being paranoid, believing that something that has never happened before is going to occur en masse the moment we don our holsters and guns. But don't take my word for it. Here it is straight from the American Heritage Dictionary.

Paranoia: Extreme, irrational distrust of others.

Don't like that one? Try the Random House Unabridged version:

Paranoia: baseless or excessive suspicion of the motives of others.

Or how about a more scientific definition?

Paranoia: a mental disorder characterized by systematized delusions and the projection of personal conflicts, which are ascribed to the supposed hostility of others.

Do any of these definitions describe CPL holders? In a word – no.

On the other hand, do any of these definitions describe the anti-gun community?

Let's break it down. Are they extreme? Yes. Are they irrational? Yes. Do they baselessly distrust us and suspect us? Absolutely! Let's be frank here. If they're really all that terrified of us, then why do they insult us at every turn? They claim that we're lunatics with guns, so if that's true, does it really make a lot of sense for them to slander our character at every turn? I don't think so.

What have we done to merit their hostile treatment? Not a thing. In fact the opposite is true. We are men and women (sheepdogs) dedicated to protecting ourselves and other innocent people from the predatory wolves in our society. We love our children. We love our spouse. We even go so far as to put our own lives in danger to protect the innocent and weak among us. How does that work? When a mugger pulls a knife on someone I love, I discourage his action with 85 grains of high-velocity lead clothed in a metal jacket. When a rapist attacks my wife – I shoot him.

Call me crazy, call me Mr. Hyde, but I'm not about to stand idly by while some lunatic kills my wife and children simply because a few extremists are paranoid. Likewise, I'm not about to stand quietly by while an overzealous politician tries to disarm me and my family. It just won't happen. I think we've been passive and polite long enough. I think we've turned the other cheek more than we should have. After all, a person only has two cheeks. In my opinion, it's time we started fighting back!

So the next time an anti-gunner starts calling you paranoid, delusional, or just flat-out crazy because you carry concealed for family defense, I want you to turn it right back on him. Don't play defense and don't be shy. Because you're not the crazy one. He is. After all, he's the one who believes that a piece of metal and plastic can turn an otherwise loving, honest person into a murderous, maniacal monster! He's also the one running around unarmed in a dangerous world. Only a lunatic would do that. Reason and sanity are on our side. We have the moral high ground. Don't ever give it up!

The Story Behind the Story

After reading the article below, you might walk away thinking "Skip Coryell believes that all anti-gun people are crazy!" And, of course, that couldn't be further from the truth. I don't think they're crazy. Well, not all of them.

All joking aside, I believe that most of them are well-intentioned people who really want the best for the world. They want to live in peace and harmony, hand in hand with all those around them. But the problem is that will never happen. People just aren't designed that way. To quote my first CPL book *"Blood in the Streets"*:

"And let's all just join hands and circle the campfire, singing endless verses of "*Kumbaya*". Oops! What's wrong with this picture? The guy holding my hand wants to steal my wallet to buy drugs. The guy 5 sheeple down wants to kidnap my son. The sixth person to my left wants to rape my wife. Hmmm, I guess maybe we can't all "just get along" after all. Reality always gets in the way of utopia, and reality will always be trump."

On the other hand, there are some anti-gunners who simply want power and control. They know that as long as we have our guns, we could stand in their way. These people will never be convinced and must continually be held in check.

No, I don't think anti-gun people are crazy, but neither do I trust their misguided idealism and their lack of good, common sense. Reality will always prevail, eventually. Even the mighty Soviet Union fell despite all its power, primarily because the reality was that people wanted freedom, and a shackled spirit can never compete with a free society. They couldn't keep up with us because their society was artificial and forced. But America was natural and free. We prevailed because our way was worth working and fighting for and theirs was not. Reality is always trump.

And the reality that this article points out is that people who legally carry concealed are honest, law-abiding citizens who are of good character and sound mind.

Seven

The Hearts and Minds of Soccer Moms

A few days ago I was giving a book signing in Iowa. About 30 people showed up and I talked for about an hour about the craft of writing. Afterwards, almost everyone there bought at least one book. It was a good day.

But the best part of the day came later as I was about to leave. A middle-aged woman stopped me and said, "I just wanted to tell you that I read your book *Blood in the Streets* and I hated it!" I was a bit surprised, interested, and somewhat amused. I looked her in the eyes, judged her character and saw a good person. I asked her, "So why did you hate reading my book?" Her answer went something like this.

"I read the first chapter and I was so disgusted that I put it down and said I would never pick it up again. I hate guns!" I nodded my head and she continued.

"But then the following week I read the second chapter, but I put it down again vowing never to read more of it." She was quiet for a moment, almost as if in agony. I stayed silent, waiting for her to finish.

"Later on I read another chapter and another and then another. Eventually, I read the whole thing and now I agree with you. We do need guns even though I hate them."

I smiled and responded. "So what did I write that kept you coming back for more?"

She smiled as well. "It was the way you kept talking about family and protecting the ones we love. And now that I've heard you in person I know that it's real. Women should be able to protect their children, even if they have to use a gun to do it."

We talked a few minutes more and then she bought another copy of the book for a friend. Afterwards, I got to thinking about the whole battle for the hearts and minds of women. I think us men just don't get it sometimes. We argue solely with our heads to the exclusion of our hearts, whereas many women focus most on their feelings. In my opinion, the right to keep and bear arms movement needs the support of women or it will never endure. Men and women need to come together, to meld their hearts and minds, their intellect and their feelings, in a show of unity and solidarity. Too many of us try to convert women to the cause using fear tactics, or constitutional arguments, when, in reality, most women don't care about that. They just want to love and be loved and to raise their children in peace and harmony. Men are quick to beat the drums of war, whereas women are the last to send their sons and daughters to fight and die. Men would do well to remember that.

When you talk to a woman about guns, don't talk about

guns. Talk about her family. Talk about her children whom she loves and reveres. In general, women take care of children more than men do, therefore they are the primary protectors of those children. They need the right tool for the job. A woman with a cell phone is no match for a criminal with a knife.

Women are just as smart and capable as men, but we have to speak their language. When you are talking to a woman about the need for CCW, always remember one thing: "The way to a woman's mind, is often through her heart."

The Story Behind the Story

I've published five books and I go to a lot of book signings all over in many different types of venues. Sure, most of my signings are at book stores, but I've also had them at churches, schools, gas stations, libraries, even one at a historic village. It seems I'll peddle my wares just about anyplace. But one thing remains constant: I'm always incredibly nervous the day before and the day of a book signing. It's a very personal and intimate thing to put your thoughts, ideas, and beliefs down on paper. It opens one up to a very profound rejection. I doubt that I'll ever like that part of my writing career. It hurts when people don't like my work. On the other hand, I understand that it's the height of arrogance to think that my own thoughts are worth other people's valuable time and money. It's a tenuous and tough sell.

So when I showed up at a library in rural Iowa, I didn't know what to expect. Frankly, half the time I never know if anyone will even show up. (As an interesting sidenote, when I was a Director for Ted Nugent United Sportsmen of America I used to work crowd control for Ted at some of his book signings. People would line up for hours just to meet him, buy a book and get his autograph. Silly me. I thought my book signings would be the same way. I suppose I should have learned to play the guitar before learning how to write.)

But on this particular day, in this simple, little Iowa town, surrounded by tall corn and down-home people, I met a woman who absolutely hated my book. And I loved it!

Eight

Land of the Semi-free – Home of the Somewhat Brave

A few days ago I went on the road with my family, on the way to my son's wedding in Wisconsin. While I love seeing my son, I hate driving to Wisconsin, because it means I must either take the long way up through the Upper Peninsula or drive through the People's Republic of Illinois. Sometimes I drive up over the bridge just to deny Illinois the pleasure of my money. It's a spiteful act, and I realize I shouldn't do it, but sometimes I just get uppity and I can't help myself.

This trip we were short on time, so I found myself taking the southern route through Indiana and into Chicago. Did I mention that I hate driving in Chicago? It's a CPL holder's nightmare. As we neared Gary, Indiana on I-94, a clump of anger welled up in my stomach, trying to work its way up into my throat. In just a few miles, I would be forced to pull off the highway and unload my pistol, lock it in my gun safe, and stow it in the back along with my liberty. There's something immoral about that.

I know some people who defy unjust and immoral laws by civil disobedience. I don't judge them for it, and I certainly understand their reasons for doing it. It's just not a decision I can recommend or choose for myself. I've always been of the belief that if you don't agree with a law, you should work and fight to have it changed. It's the American way, and it's the basis of our political system and the lifeblood that flows through our great country. In America, if you don't like something, you can change it. Where else in the world can you do that? America is indeed a special place.

As you recall, I lived in Iowa the entire year of 2007. Iowa CPL (they call is CCW there) is different than ours. They have a patchwork quilt system of "may issue" which, quite frankly, just doesn't work. There are 99 counties in Iowa and the County Sheriff has sole power to either grant or deny a CCW permit. Before moving to Iowa, I logged on to a website called www.iowacarry.org and looked at their "red-yellow-green" map to see which counties issued permits and which did not. I had to live within a green county to get my permit, but I still had to be close enough to Cedar Rapids for my wife to drive to work. We ended up in Jones County where Sheriff Mark Denniston was more than happy to issue me a permit. Not only did he waive the training requirements for me, but he also enlisted me to teach the county CCW classes. Five hundred miles from home I had found a kindred RKBA spirit. Even though I've moved back to Michigan, Mark and I stay in touch, and I'm still active in Iowa's battle for "shall issue" CCW. They came close this past year, and

I expect next year could be the right time for them. Let's hope, work, and pray that their battle pays off.

I remember that every month, when I drove back from Iowa to Michigan to teach a CPL class, I would dread driving down I-80 up to the state border, because I knew that once I crossed the mighty Mississippi, I would be entering RKBA enemy territory. I always waited until the last mile, then I'd pull into the rest stop and stow my pistol. Then I'd gas up, buy a large Frappuccino, and drive 2 miles below the speed limit all the way through the People's Republic of Illinois, and through the south end of Chicago. I would count down the miles to free soil - Indiana, land of the free and home of the brave. Then I'd pull over just across the border and tool-up for self defense once again.

Why do I feel more free when I'm carrying a pistol? The answer is quite simple. I feel more free, because I am more free.

I have relatives in southern Illinois, and they come from good American stock: farmers, hunters, and gun owning sportsmen. I went down to visit with them once and we talked about the right to keep and bear arms. My relative showed me his Illinois Firearm Owners Identification Card. What a sad state when you have to get permission from the government simply to own a gun. I felt sorry for him, because he had no idea how shackled he'd become. Over the decades, Illinois has been transformed by liberal Chicago politics from a once-proud state into the land of the semi-free and the home of the somewhat brave.

And I don't mean that as a slam to the good people of Illinois, because my feelings are more sympathetic than anything else. While there is spite in my heart for the government of Illinois, there is nothing but genuine sorrow for its people. They are more subject than citizen now.

But even now, as I drive south through Wisconsin toward the People's Republic of Illinois (both states are lands of shackled subjects) I harbor true hope in my heart, knowing that there are thousands of people here fighting desperately to regain the constitutional right to keep and bear arms for themselves and their children. We should help them as much as we can.

I realize all too well, that now, even as I write this article, I too am a subservient subject. I am subject to the laws of the People's Republic of Wisconsin and, in a few more hours, the People's Republic of Illinois. Even though their laws are unconstitutional, immoral, and unjust, I must obey them – at least as long as the political means are there to make the wrong things right. The governments of Illinois and Wisconsin have long been insults to our founding fathers and American Freedom.

But in five more hours, I'll be a free man again. I'll roll into Indiana, I'll tool up, gas up, and buy my Frappuccino. A few hours later, my home state of Michigan, that giant, freedom-filled blue mitten, will appear in my windshield. I'll be home again, free again, knowing in my heart that I'm once again more citizen than subject. I understand that my liberty is a gift of the people who came before me, and who fought on my behalf. Even now, we still fight on desperately in a never-ending battle to keep the political shacklers at bay. Always remember: it's not about guns, it's about control. And subjects are controlled, but citizens are free. Free to control their own destiny.

Please do all you can to help our RKBA brothers and sisters

in Illinois, Iowa, and Wisconsin to regain their freedoms. Always remember, that no one is free, until all of us are free. Semi-free and somewhat brave is not good enough. America is better than that.

I encourage you to log on to the following websites and donate to the cause:

www.iowacarry.org

www.wisconsinconcealedcarry.com

www.isra.

The Story Behind the Story

When I was writing this article, I did so knowing that I was going to get a few negative emails. But that's okay. At least I know that people are reading my work and that I'm moving them to action, even if it is a bit critical. That's probably one of the most distasteful things about writing a column. I just don't take criticism well. I think deep down inside I must suffer from low self-esteem. I had one person write me the following:

> "I too live in Michigan and I know that it is NOT the bastion of freedom your words indicate. It is better by comparison to Illinois or Wisconsin - indeed. But what if we compare it to Vermont or Alaska - then pray-tell we fare not well and indeed we too fall under the condemning eye of the Founding Fathers of our country."

Of course the man is right on all counts. But all of us already knew that. Everything is relative. It was nice to get his email though.

Another man, a Warrant Officer in the military, also had a valid complaint:

> "I enjoy reading your articles in the MCRGO but do disagree on one point. I don't see MI entirely as not also being a People's Republic. When I as a Michigan Native and voting resident on Active Duty cross the border into MI on family visits I must pull off to the side of the road and lock my freedom in the trunk. When the military moved me to VA and my MI CPL expired, MI denied my renewal application stating I was no longer a resident. I have a VA resident CCW permit even though I carry a Michigan Drivers license, voters registration and vehicle registration.
>
> Attorney General Cox has advised me that my FL, VA, and NH permits don't grant me the right to carry in MI because I have a MI drivers license."

This was a sad email to read, particularly because we have a Michigan native, on active duty, being denied his right to keep and bear arms. I sent this one on to a State Representative and will do my best to restore the freedom that he has vowed to protect and defend on our behalf.

Freedom is relative. It shouldn't be - but it is. That's why all of us have to get active in politics, even though politics can be dirty, time-consuming and distasteful. There are differing levels of liberty all across our country. The people who work the hardest to restore their freedoms usually get the payoff. The moral of the story is, get involved, work hard, don't sit on the fence and let others work for you.

Nine

The Madman's got a Gun!

There's a madman running around out there in Michigan, and he's a got a gun – a big one – and he pays no attention to pistol-free zones. But you don't need to worry about him shooting up a school or a church or even a daycare center. Why? Because he's not your everyday, garden variety, run-of-the-mill madman. This madman is special. He's Ted Nugent, the Motor City Madman, and he's touring this great country of ours on a nonstop speaking tour giving a speech titled *God, Guns, and Rock-n-Roll*! And what's more, he'll be speaking right here in Michigan at Western Michigan University on Monday, March 31st. The venue is 7PM at Miller Auditorium and the speech is open to the public and free of charge.

My first exposure to Ted was watching him on television when his PBS *Spirit of the Wild* series aired many years ago. I remember thinking "Hey, that guy makes a lot of sense." The next day I called the phone number on the screen and joined Ted Nugent

United Sportsmen of America (then called Ted Nugent World Bowhunters). Over the ensuing decade, I became a director in his organization and eventually rose to the position of Michigan State Director. Serving in that capacity, I got to know Ted and his family quite well.

One thing that I learned very quickly, was that Ted Nugent casts a very long shadow. In fact, I've been standing in that shadow for many years now, basking in his mentorship, learning how to stand up and shoot back (in the rhetorical sense) whenever anti-gunners pop their furry little heads up out of their burrows. There are several things about Ted that are indisputable: he doesn't play defense; he doesn't take prisoners; his logic is unassailable; his confidence is brazen; and his uncanny grasp of the issues and the facts is downright scary.

As for myself, boy could I tell you some stories about the madman - but I'm not going to - perhaps another time. But here's what I will tell you: Ted Nugent, AKA the Motor City Madman, the Teditor Predator, Uncle Ted, the Nuge, whatever you want to call him, Ted Nugent is a WYSIWYG man. That's a computer acronym which means "What You See Is What You Get". Ted is the same person everywhere he goes whether it's around a campfire, rocking on stage, or at home with his family. Once, before I knew him better, I asked Ted about his "rock-n-roll persona". His reply seemed abrupt and a bit impatient as if he was talking to a young buck who needed his butt kicked. "I have no persona!" he told me. And now that I've known him all these years, I know better than to ask stupid questions like that.

And yet, Ted Nugent is the kind of guy who inspires either

undying loyalty and devotion or extreme hatred and fear. There is no middle ground when it comes to the Motor City Madman. People either love him or they hate him. Ted's world is kind of like a cut and dried, black and white camo pattern.

So, here I am, a success in my own right: an author of five books, a motivational speaker, and a sought-after personal defense instructor. But still, after more than a decade, I continue to stand in Ted's shadow. But, quite frankly folks, I wouldn't have it any other way. There's a lot to be said about the shade, especially on a hot, sunny day. Ted Nugent, with his in-your-face style, his brashness, and his no-compromise full throttle, no apologies stand for the Second Amendment, he takes a lot of heat off the rest of us. So I'm really quite content to stand in his legendary shadow, much the same way he stood in the shadow of own father while growing up, and then later with his mentor Fred Bear.

All of us have heroes. All of us stand in someone else's shadow. But the nice thing is, we get to choose where we stand. Now, I have no doubt this commentary will generate a few irate emails, but I'm okay with that. Some of you will complain: "But he's rude! He's brash! He's loud!" To which I respond: "Well, yes, he's Ted! How do you expect a madman to act? Civilized? I think not."

Ted is more constant than water. He doesn't change from liquid to vapor to solid, depending on his environment. Ted is a WYSIWYG man. What you see is what you get. And I find that incredibly refreshing, especially in the world of politics.

If I could bottle Ted Nugent, then I would pass out an ounce of him with every book I sell. Because I think the world can use a little more Ted and a lot less Chuck Schumer and Teddy Kennedy.

And now I leave you with a sneak preview of Ted's upcoming speech titled "God, Guns, and Rock-n-roll". It came straight from his computer to mine and I share it now in hopes that a little bit of Ted's true north brashness will rub off onto your spirit, infusing you with courage, boldness and power.

"I know free men. I work, play, hunt, fish, rock and hang with free men everyday. We know in our hearts and souls that God gave us the sacred gift of life, and with this sacred gift comes the self-evident truth that we have the God given right and spiritual duty to defend that gift. KEEP means "it is mine, you can't have it". BEAR means "yes, I have it right here on me". SHALL NOT BE INFRINGED is not ambiguous. It means "don't tread on me". We the people of this great experiment in self-government must eliminate all these offensive infringements on our God given, US Constitutionally guaranteed rights immediately. That the worse slaughters of innocent lives have occurred in "gun free zones" is an outrage that all good American families must fight hard to eradicate. America must ban gun free zones now. No more forcibly unarmed helpless sheep to slaughter! We rally for good over evil, not the gun-free zone guarantee of evil over good. Now more than ever. God bless America, God bless freedom."

There, now you've had your ounce of Ted. If you can handle more, show up at his speech. I know I will. I'll be the one backstage, basking in the coolness of his shadow. I hope to see many other MCRGO members there as well. God bless.

Author's Note: Since this article was written, Ted Nugent has published his next book titled "*Ted, White, and Blue*". It is currently in the top ten on the New York Times bestseller list. You can order your copy from tednugent.com. I highly recommend it.

The Story Behind the Story

Most of you know that I'm friends with Ted Nugent and that I used to be a Director for his organization, Ted Nugent United Sportsmen of America. In that capacity, I got to know him and his family better. They are good people.

But one thing I always hated was others who befriended me just so they could get close to Ted. After a while I could sense when someone was doing it and I'd just steer clear of those people. We always called them "Tedheads".

I recall one time I received a letter from a group that wanted Ted to donate $250,000 so they could clean up the Kalamazoo River. At first glance it sounded worthwhile, though outrageously pricey. Once I looked into the group they explained to me that they were a gay and lesbian organization and wanted to use the cleanup in order to promote the homosexual lifestyle. I just couldn't see an alpha male like Ted getting involved with a gay group, so I politely declined their generous offer. It seems there was always someone trying to part Ted from his money.

Another thing I hated, and sometimes this still happens, is

that every time Ted says something outrageous, a few people call to me and complain. They always start by telling me they love him but that he shouldn't be so loud and outrageous. Hello! Excuse me! This is Ted Nugent we're talking about. You can't put a lion in a cage; you can't predict the wind. Just let it go. Either love him or hate him. But the choice is always yours.

The above article was written for two publications: the MCRGO Newsletter and tednugent.com. It appeared the week before Ted's speech at Western Michigan University.

Ten

A Question of Courage

I have long believed that the fate of the Second Amendment ultimately lies in the hands of women, so Jeanne Assam is a comforting ray of hope for me. Let's face it, the women outnumber us men, so if they don't support the right to keep and bear arms, then it could well fall idly onto the ash heap of history as a good idea that just didn't stand the test of time. We can't let that happen.

Gun ownership by women is on the rise in this country. As an NRA concealed carry instructor, I can tell you that 6 years ago only 10 percent of my students were women, but now that number has risen to about 25 percent. And this pleases me. We need more women shooters. In my experience, they tend to become better shots than many of the men. After all, accuracy is 90 percent trigger pull, and women have a much gentler touch than us clumsy, meat-handed men.

I remember last week when I first heard the news of the

Omaha Mall shootings. My first thought was "Oh no. Here we go again. The crazies will be out in force." And they were. I told myself I would not write an article about that shooting. I find it depressing to constantly pour over all the details in dozens of news articles about deranged killers shooting innocent men, women and children with impunity. So, despite the fact that others expected me to speak out, I kept silent. It was a short-lived pen-slinger sabbatical.

But there's one thing I recall about last week's news coverage that stunned me. I was listening to a female reporter interview a middle-aged woman who had been in the mall during the shootings.

Reporter: So what did you do when you heard the shots and realized that people were dying?

Woman at Mall: I ran back into the store. I got as far back as possible, and then hid inside a closet.

Reporter: Well thank you very much for your time. You are a very brave woman.

Woman at Mall: I didn't feel brave. I was terrified.

There's a reason she didn't feel brave; it's because she wasn't. She was a sheep. And there's no shame in that so long as you're willing to face the fate of a sheep. In my book *Blood in the Streets* I make the following statement:

"Sheep are born and bred for one purpose: to be killed and to have their parts processed into something useful by predators. They stand on the hill and go "Baa", as they're being slaughtered."

Jeanne Assam is a woman, but she is certainly no sheep.

Not many news sources are reporting this, so few of us realize that there was not one, but two armed security guards confronting the shooter at the entrance to New Life Community Church. There were two worshippers who drew their firearms that day, but only one who was able to advance forward and gun down the man who hated Christians and who had vowed to kill as many as he possibly could. It was a woman, Jeanne Assam, who stepped out from the safety of cover and advanced toward the heavily armed shooter. He shot at her three times but she continued to advance all the while yelling for him to surrender and returning fire. As in most mass shootings, the killer turned the gun on himself as soon as he was met with a determined citizen with equal force. She stopped the deranged murderer, not just with bullets, but also with love and with courage. And she did so with unflinching courage and resolve with no regard for her own safety.

In the light of all that's happened, I respectfully submit that courage is not defined by one's gender, but by one's actions. We need more women to carry pistols. It would appear that there just aren't enough brave people out there who are ready, willing and able to stand guard over the flock. Jeanne Assam may have been afraid, but she overcame that fear with love for the innocent sheep she was tasked to protect. She confronted the wolf and said, "no more – you shall not pass" and then she put him down. Without fear, there is little opportunity for courage.

When my wife heard that the hero was a woman, she smiled and raised her right hand up for me to give her a high five. She said, "Yes! Way to go!" Women need heroes as much as men, and when that hero is a woman, then it's all the more inspiring and empowering to them. Men, it's time to step up. Yes, I'm a strong and able concealed carry instructor. I'm a hunter, an outdoorsman, and a Marine. But today gents – my hero is a woman!

And I have three words for all you pistol-packin' women out there: You go girl!

The Story Behind the Story

It was 9 December 2007 and I heard pieces of a radio news report saying that a YWAM base had just been visited by an unknown gunman and that 4 people had been shot. I was immediately terrified, because my oldest son, Chris, is on staff at the YWAM base in northern Wisconsin. YWAM stands for Youth with a Mission. It is a Christian organization that trains young people in the basics of the Christian faith, then sends them to do short-term mission work in other countries. I was terrified for my son. Was it him? Was he okay or was he already dead. I called but couldn't get through and that made matters worse.

For several minutes I searched the internet for news and listened to the radio. Eventually, I found out he was okay. It was the YWAM base in Arvada, Colorado. I was relieved.

But then only 12 hours later, the same gunman walked into the New Life Community Church in Colorado Springs and started shooting. He carried with him 2 hand guns, a rifle, and over 1,000 rounds of ammunition. The gunman shot 5 people in the parking lot before coming inside the church. Once there, he was met by a woman with a gun.

"There was chaos," Assam said. "I will never forget the

gunshots. They were so loud."

"I saw him coming through the doors" and took cover, Assam said. "I came out of cover and identified myself and engaged him and took him down."

"God was with me," Assam said. "I didn't think for a minute to run away."

Those are the words of RKBA hero Jeanne Assam who met the gunman near the entrance of the church, identified herself, ordered him to stop and then shot and killed him. It is estimated that she saved 50 to 100 lives. There were about 7,000 people on the church campus at the time of the shooting.

The above article was published on tednugent.com and in the MCRGO newsletter as well as in Concealed Carry magazine.

Eleven

Doing the Lord's Work

"**A**men! Brother! Preach it!"

People were shouting, clapping, and raising their hands to the sky, some sitting in the pews, others standing, but if there had been decent aisles they surely would have rolled on down with all the fervor one finds on a Sunday morning in an all-black church below the Mason-Dixon Line! It was a good day to give the devils some hell!

But I wasn't in the deep south, not by a long shot. I wasn't even in a building with a steeple. I was riveted to my pew, cocked, locked and ready to rock, deep within the bowels of Miller Auditorium at Western Michigan University. I was sitting in reverence and shock and awe, studying the doctrine of common sense, worshipping under the tutelage of the greatest fire and brimstone preacher of our time. No, it wasn't Billy Graham and it sure as hell wasn't the Reverend Al Sharpton. It was the mighty Reverend Ted Nugent and I was basking in the warmth and glowfire of the First Nugent Church of Sonic Bombast and God, Guns, and Rock-n-roll!

The Reverend Nugent paced back and forth across the front of the stage like a caged animal in heat! He would not be denied and his voice would not be silenced!

"You're either in the asset column of America or the liability column. I've been in the asset column ever since 1948. Sometimes my dad had to force me to be there, but I was always there. In the asset column you've got a clean, healthy lifestyle, you've got the ten commandments and family and serving your country. In the liability column you've got smoking, alcohol, drugs and people sleeping in and collecting a welfare check! But I say if you don't work then you don't eat! I say that every able-bodied person in this country should get off their fat ass and, dare I say it? Get a fucking job!"

The congregation erupted into applause once more and the Reverend Nugent paused to wait them out. But he didn't wait too long, because tonight his timing was perfect; his wit was sharp and cutting like a Grizzly bear's claw, and he didn't want to give the parishioners time to rest. Tonight, the Reverend Madman was in true form; he was picture-perfect; he was an All-American conservative icon with tooth, fang and claw. He was Norman Rockwell with an attitude!

"And then you've got the Supremes in their holy, black robes who have the audacity and the ignorance to debate whether or not we have the individual God-given right to keep and bear arms! Now, folks, I'm just a guitar player, but I know free men. I work, play, hunt, fish, rock and hang with free men everyday. We know in our hearts and souls that God gave us the sacred gift of life, and with this sacred gift comes the self-evident truth that we have the God-given right and spiritual duty to defend that gift. KEEP means "it is mine, you can't have it".

Once again ear-thumping applause boomed out as if on cue. I was in the front row, on the edge of the pew, leaning on every word. The adrenaline was pumping like liquid iron through my veins imbuing me with courage, reminding me that once upon a time this country was free. Finally, the applause died down and Pastor Nugent continued with renewed fervor.

"BEAR means "yes, I have it right here on me! All the time!"

More applause and Ted tapped the omnipresent Brother Kimber on his strong side.

"SHALL NOT BE INFRINGED is not ambiguous. It means don't tread on me! It means leave me alone!"

Even louder applause!

"And now a word about these stupid gun-free zones. Oh, by the way, did I mention that before I walked in the room this place was a gun-free zone?"

The reverend paused for effect and grinned that patented Cheshire-cat-scratch-fever-like smile of his before moving in for the kill, no pun intended.

"That the worse slaughters of innocent lives have occurred in "gun free zones" is an outrage that all good American families must fight hard to eradicate. America must ban gun free zones now! No more forcibly unarmed helpless sheep to slaughter! We rally for good over evil, not the gun free zone guarantee of evil over good. We the people are the National Rifle Association and the Second Amendment IS our concealed weapons permit!"

The applause erupted even louder than before. My ears were ringing and my heart was working overtime to force the new-found liquid iron through my body. A sudden sadness followed by immediate anger swept over me as I looked down at my strong side, now rendered weak and impotent. I felt the empty holster beneath my shirt and knew, at that moment, that I had been forcibly disarmed by the senseless laws of a liberal legislature and the so-called conservatives without the backbone and intelligence to prevail against them. Before entering the auditorium, I had unloaded my Smith and Wesson MP 9 millimeter and left it unattended in the car. And then the reality of my predicament swept over me like a wave of True North magma, burning my heart and searing itself forever into my soul: "In order to remain an honest, law-abiding citizen, my elected leaders had disarmed me, in essence transforming me into a mere serf, a subject, a vassal and ward of the state, depending upon them for the very life-blood that flowed through my veins. Without my gun, I was at their mercy. Suddenly, I no longer trusted them, not even their so-called "good intentions". Just as the leaders of the Spanish Inquisition had abused their self-proclaimed God-given author-ity, so had our own legislators abused their responsibility to serve us, the citizens, we the people of this great country.

When the Reverend Nugent closed his sermon over 2 hours

after it began, he lifted us up, exhorting us to new heights, challenging us to press on in the fight.

> "In summary, let me tell you that we all have a lot of work to do. We have to take this state back, and we have to take this country back. We have to write letters to our Congressmen and to the media, and we have to tell them we're not going to take this bullshit any longer! Aside from that we all have friends and family who don't vote or who don't believe in our rights. Talk to them. Speak out! Let them know how you feel about it!"

As the applause erupted again, I realized that Ted Nugent was more than just a cultural icon, more than a rock star, and more than just a reverend with an axe to grind. He was a prophet, like the ones of old, imploring us to return to the principles of God, Family and Country. His words, and the steel visage of his face and courage reminded me of the words of God to the wisest man on earth, King Solomon: "If my people, who are called by my name, shall humble themselves and pray, and seek my face, and turn from their wicked ways, then will I hear from heaven and will forgive their sin and I will heal their land."

Last night, the secular brick, mortar and stone of Miller auditorium was consecrated, was set apart for a more holy purpose, it was honored with a message from God – a message that could very well save America. "The pimps, whores, and welfare brats; the chimps who have taken over the asylum, threatening to forever transform our great world into the planet of the apes must be opposed and defeated with every breath and molecule we possess. There is no excuse. We've been forewarned.

And now, as I sit safely in my living room, with my Smith and Wesson at my side as loyal as a hunting dog, I tell you that it's up to each one of us to heed the call and do the right thing. Now, Godspeed to you and stop caring what liberal idiots think about you. Roll up your sleeves, say a prayer and TAKE OUR NATION BACK!

Praise the Lord, and pass the ammunition!

The Story Behind the Story

I remember writing this story specifically for Ted Nugent. He liked it so much that he placed it on the home page of tednugent. com. From there it went to websites, emails, and talk forums all over the worldwide web. Most people enjoyed it, but the ones who hated it - really hated it! But then Ted has always been a polarizing figure.

I went to the speech with Barry County Sheriff Dar Leaf. Dar is a long-time friend and fellow NRA Instructor. He teaches all the legal portions of my basic concealed carry classes. Before the speech we were invited back stage to talk to Ted and have a photo taken with him. Ever since Ted bought that ranch in Texas, I haven't gotten to see him as often.

Ted's speech was blistering and rated R for rude, righteous, and railing. It was the best civics sermon I've ever heard. Too bad our high schools couldn't tape it and show it to all our kids. It would make them much better citizens.

Afterwards, Dar and I stopped off at a McDonald's for a bite to eat. We were excited and chatted away about the tenacity and candor of Ted's speech.

I remember saying to Dar "It makes me mad that I had to keep my pistol locked up in your car. I'm glad you were there. At least one of us was packing."

Dar got a sheepish look on his face and I asked him "What's wrong." He answered "Promise not to tell anyone, but I ran off without my pistol. I'm unarmed."

I laughed out loud. Imagine that, a Sheriff and NRA Training Counselor going to see Ted Nugent without a pistol. Needless to say, I never promised I would keep my mouth shut about his embarrassing little secret.

Probably the highlight of the evening for me was when Ted mentioned my name on stage. I'm no Tedhead, but I was proud, nonetheless. It was a good night with the Reverend Nugent, one I'll never forget. Hope you enjoyed the article.

Twelve

Taking out the Trash

Last weekend I was in Southwest Michigan teaching a CPL class to 15 students. My partner and co-owner of Midwest Tactical Training (www.mwtac.com) Larry Jackson, was up front teaching the NRA's four levels of awareness. They are, quite simply, "unaware, aware, alert, and alarm". One of our students raised his hand and said, "I don't think I want to live that way." Larry asked the student (his name was Bill) why he felt that way, and his answer was really quite thought provoking and eloquent.

> "I don't want to live that way, because I think it would drive me crazy. I'm afraid of spending so much time looking out for bad guys that I lose sight of the good things in life, like my wife, the most wonderful person in the world. I don't want to be so concerned about evil that I miss all the good things in life."

Larry and Bill went back and forth a few times, and then I

stood up and responded in an attempt to allay his fears. I said, "Bill, being aware of your surroundings is not an emotional act that consumes you. It has nothing to do with emotions at all. It's a matter of balance and practice. After a while, you do it without even thinking about it."

I've long believed that most of personal and family defense has little to do with firearms. Like all of us say "A firearm is a tool of last resort". We carry the tool as a "just in case" insurance policy. However, if we do have to clear leather, then chances are we may have fallen short in other areas. Perhaps we unnecessarily frequented a bad neighborhood. Perhaps we challenged when we should have backed off. Perhaps we chose the "wrong" friends. Never underestimate the power of the best form of self defense: a smile and a kind word. But most of the potential altercations we face can be averted by a sharp mind, that is constantly aware of our surroundings.

Retired Police Officer, Dave Spaulding, wrote a great article about it called "*What Really Happens in a Gunfight?*" In the article, Mr. Spaulding talks about interviewing over 200 survivors of gun fights, some law enforcement, some military, and some civilian. It was interesting to note that many of the "winners" (spelled "survivors") of gunfights were not caught off guard. They had taken the time to prepare by practicing with their firearm, participating in shooting competition, routinely using visualization techniques, and by staying aware of their surroundings. All these things combined to shorten their "startle response" time. Startle response is simply the length of time it takes you to respond to a violent encounter.

As a former Marine, I understand that the best advantage in any battle is the element of surprise. Throughout history, the element of surprise has been the deciding factor in all kinds of battles. When that mugger jumps out from behind a bush and waves a knife in your face, he expects you to submit. Why? Because this is not his first time. He has mugged many people and has never been resisted. The element of surprise is on his side. Most common, non-CPL holding people (most sheep) are defenseless to resist, so they wet their pants instead and have no choice but to trust to the good nature of a recidivistic madman who may or may not kill them. That's not good enough for me.

I'm not going to get into exactly "how" to respond in such an attack for two reasons: 1) it's beyond the scope of the article, 2) I could never cover it sufficiently on paper. There are just way too many unknown and changing variables in a violent attack. This type of training should occur in person.

But this much I can safely tell you: Awareness and preparedness is the foundation of self defense. Whether you fight or whether you flee, your response should be predetermined and immediate. It will be more difficult to kill a person who is prepared and expecting a fight. When your startle response is nil, the element of surprise shifts from the bad guy to you and your chances of survival are significantly improved.

Practicing the four levels of awareness: unaware, aware, alert, and alarm, is something you should do out of habit, like looking in your rear-view mirror before changing lanes. It's a common-sense safety issue. It's a fact of life that we live in a dangerous world. It's like taking out the trash every Tuesday morning before heading off to work. We don't do it because we like it or because it's fun. We do it because the trash is there and it needs to be taken out or it will adversely affect our lives.

I remember many years ago after getting out of boot camp, that whenever I visited the mall or went into a room with dozens of people, I was a nervous wreck. I was always on full alert, trying to watch everyone at the same time. It was an impossible task, and I soon learned that balance in my life was key to survival and to happiness. I toned it down.

On the other hand, we don't want to take the ostrich route, denying that evil exists and is a danger to us. We don't want to bury our heads in the sand. If we live long enough, our luck will run out and that can only end in one way: a body-shaped chalk line.

"Stay Alert – Stay Alive": anyone familiar with self defense and the military mindset knows that this mantra was repeated many times by the late Colonel David H. Hackworth, God rest his soul. He was a true American warrior, and he lived what he preached. So do I. And so should you. Ninety percent of personal defense is what we do "before" the attack occurs. Get prepared, stay aware. Stay alert – stay alive. It's not an emotional thing. It's just taking out the trash.

The Story Behind the Story

I always tell my concealed carry students that ninety percent of personal protection has nothing to do with your firearm. Yes, I always carry my firearm and so should you. But there is no good substitute for a sharpened mind, well prepared, well trained and ready for a fight. I practice the self defense technique of visualization on a daily basis. It's gotten to be such a discipline that I doubt I could stop it if I tried.

Every once in a while my wife will say to me "Are you listening to me?" (To many spouses that is the wedded kiss of death.) Inside I say "Oops! I didn't hear a word." In my younger days I'd be tempted to try and talk my way out of it, but later in life I learned that the best course of action was just to fess up and take my medicine. So I say "Sorry honey. I was thinking." Of course then her next question is "What were you thinking about?"

That reminds me of a sitcom where the wife asks her husband that same question. The husband unwisely answers: "If I wanted you to know what I was thinking, then I'd be talking instead of thinking."

Instead I tell her the truth. "I'm sorry honey, but I just daydreamed that a man walked in here with a gun to rob the place. But it's okay. I shot him and now he's gone."

My wife has grown used to this response so she simply says "Okay. Thank you honey." Hence, the marital crisis is averted.

Am I always on full alert status? No, of course not. No one can do that without going crazy. But I do my best, and so far my best has been good enough. If you do nothing else, even if you don't carry a pistol, always stay alert.

Thirteen

I'm not Dead Yet!

A few months ago I received a most generous offer to join the American Association of Retired People (AARP). Disgusted, I tore it up and threw it away. The following week, I received another one. I threw that one away too. But they just kept sending them. Apparently, someone thinks I'm no longer young. How can that be? I'm only 50 years old. Oops! Did I just say "50 years old"?

The next day, I stood in front of the mirror after my shower for an honest, objective evaluation. There are wrinkles around my eyes; my hairline is receding towards the back of my head like a puddle drying in the hot summer sun; as if on cue, bushy follicles are growing in my ears, nose and on my back. Thirty years ago I was a United States Marine. My torso rippled with lean muscle and I routinely did 25 one-handed pushups with both arms just because I could.

Life is not fair. Just when I become wise enough and economically advantaged enough to enjoy life, my body falls apart. I feel like my physique has gone AWOL and I don't much like it!

So what does this have to do with personal protection? Everything! I am quickly becoming one of the weaker animals in the herd, and every wolf within 50 miles is checking me out to see if I'm an easy prey. I find it frustrating and very disconcerting. I suspect that my feelings are common with baby boomers. Yesterday I taught a CPL class and half of them were my age or older.

When a wolf watches the caribou herd, he instinctively knows who is old and weak, and he waits for them to lag behind. Once they are alone, the pack pounces and has its fill. But I'm not quite ready to be eaten and neither are the other "elderly" CPL holders I taught yesterday. Many of my students are in their sixties and seventies and some even in their eighties. I find hope and inspiration in their indomitable effort, and in their resilience and unwilling determination to stay one step ahead of the wolf. They won't go down without a fight and neither will I!

I am heartened by headlines such as this from Plantation, Florida:

"Retired U.S. Marine Disrupts Robbery"

According to the article, two "young", armed men attempted to rob a Subway sandwich shop. When these young whippersnappers (21 and 22 years old) tried to force 71-year-old John Lovell into the bathroom, he pulled out a gun and shot both men, one in the head and the other in the chest. One died and the other was found hiding in the bushes barely clinging to his life. Once again, God created men, but Samuel Colt made them equal.

Here's another article that caught my eye:

"72 Year Old Former Marine Beats up Pickpocket"

Bill Barnes was buying a lottery ticket at a convenience store when a "young" (27 years old) thief tried to steal his wallet. Did old Bill cry foul and cower in a corner waiting for the police to arrive? Not on your life! Weak, decrepit old Bill turned and beat the crap out of the man, pummeling him with seven punches before the store manager could intervene and rescue the thief. Check it out on YouTube. It's a breath of fresh air.

Men like Bill and John are my heroes, because they never give up. Even though the wolf is at the door, they calmly say "Come on in youngster. Let me teach you a thing or two." I can relate to them both. In my head, I realize what time is doing to me. I'm on the downhill side of my life, and my body is very slowly dying. But in my heart, I still feel like the 20-year-old Marine doing one-handed pushups. The conflict between my heart and my head is an amazing and wonderful contradiction.

I'm 50 years old, while my wife is 31 and my youngest child will turn 2 next month. While many men my age are content to sit on the porch in the rocker, bouncing their grandkids on their knees, I find myself fighting Father Time with all my heart and getting ready to pop out more puppies. Although I can see the wolves out on the fringe of the herd, watching me, waiting, looking for any sign of weakness, I stand and I defiantly say "Come on in boys. I may be old, but I'm not a caribou. I'm a man. And I'm packing a nine millimeter with +P ammo and plenty of it."

I want to encourage all of you "elderly" folks out there to resist the toll of time for as long as you can. Don't give in to it without a fight. There's still plenty of fun to be had out there, so go ahead and buy that motor home and tour the country. Don't be afraid of the wolves. Instead, look them straight in the eye like the man or woman you used to be and say "Go ahead punk! Make my day!"

We may be old, but we're not dead yet! Get trained! Get armed! Stay alert and stay alive – for many more years to come.

The Story Behind the Story

I got a lot of email response on this. All of it was positive encouragement and compliments from other aging baby boomers. One man told me:

"That is a good piece.... insightful, relevant and also the truth. Today I head for an MRI; spine problems / pain and numbness in one arm and hand. I can't play any of my (5) six string basses and my 2" groups @ 50' with a 1911 are now 7" groups. To put it bluntly this sucks, but as you so eloquently put it, "I'm not dead yet"!
Thanks Skip. Good work."

I can now confirm that misery does indeed love company.

Another man wrote:

"As a young man, I stubbornly insisted that my way was the right way, but I've mellowed with age, and can now appreciate that this is not going to happen. There are sheep, there are sheep dogs - and there will always be wolves. Your writing has reinforced that fact (and many others) in my mind, and served as a valuable link in my journey back to being an active member of an armed society."

William Faulkner once said:

"The primary job that any writer faces is to tell a story, a story out of human experience- I mean by that, universal mutual experience, the anguish and troubles and griefs of the human heart, which is universal without regard to race or time or condition."

The article "*I'm Not dead Yet*" is my story of growing old, but it's not just my story - it's everyone's story - a story that we all, someday must live out either in fluid grace or in clumsy disbelief.

I love the positive, encouraging emails, the ones I write that strike a universal chord within the heart and soul of man and woman. It makes it all worthwhile to know that I can affect positive change in people's lives ... even in my old age.

As soon as Ted Nugent walked in the room, it ceased to be a pistol-free zone. This picture was taken back stage at Western Michigan University in Kalamazoo, Michigan. Ted gave a profoundly outrageous speech titled *"God, Guns, and Rock-n-Roll"*. I have been Ted's friend for many years, and there is no greater patriot than the Nuge. He stands up to the anti-gunners like no one else can, and he makes them all look silly.

This picture was taken in Chicago, Illinois at a class taught by Massad Ayoob called "*Judicious Use of Deadly Force*". It was 20 hours of intensive training on the legal and emotional ramifications of being involved in a lethal shoot-out. Massad's Lethal Force Institute gives some of the best training in the world. You should make time to train with Massad. Massad is the master. (Go to www.ayoob.com for info on his classes.) Two friends and Lethal Force Instructors, Bob Houzenga and Andy Kemp, are kneeling in the front row.

Massad is kneeling in the number one spot and I am standing behind him. Andy and Bob are kneeling in the number 4 and 5 positions, respectively.

Four of the original RKBA rebels of Barry County are pictured here. Left to right: Sheriff Dar Leaf, Skip Coryell, Walt Herwath, and Dave Stevens. All of us worked hard, putting our reputations on the line to advance concealed carry in Michigan long before it was popular to do so. We've been in the RKBA trenches together and that's a bond that lasts a lifetime.

This picture was taken in Delton, Michigan at a charity golf outing. I golfed with the Sheriff and we had a great time despite our high scores. Tiger Woods has nothing to fear from anyone in this picture.

Roger Burdette (left) is a registered lobbyist in Des Moines for IowaCarry, Inc. He is a member of the Board of Directors and a tireless supporter for the right to keep and bear arms in Iowa. Here he is shown with State Representative Clel Baudler (right). The honorable Mr. Baudler has introduced several pro-CCW bills into the House but the climate is not yet right for passage. When the shall-issue bill is passed into law in Iowa, it will be the result of hard work by a team of dedicated individuals composed of citizen activists like IowaCarry Inc., elected officials like Representative Clel Baudler, and law enforcement supporters such as Sheriff Mark Denniston in Jones County.

We lived in Iowa only one year, but it was enough to spoil me for a lifetime. The bucks are huge and plentiful. Look at the high rack on this one, and it was considered by the locals to be a bit on the "small" side. My neighbor across the Wapsi River let me hunt his 500 acres of river bottom and timber land. It was prime white-tail habitat, and I hunted it all by myself all through bow season. The things I do for my country!

The week following the Virginia Tech Massacre, Steve Deace of WHO radio, 1040 AM, in Des Moines invited me to be a guest on his afternoon drive show and I graciously accepted. Steve talked to me about my views on gun control and personal defense, and we hit it off well from the start. Steve had me on his show three times in 2007 and we had a good time talking about the right to keep and bear arms. I am pleased to now call him my friend and fellow Christian brother. Go to www.whoradio.com and check out Steve's own book "*Without a Vision the People Perish*". It's an excellent read and I highly recommend it.

Pictured here are some of my family and friends at a book signing in Menomonie, Wisconsin. My daughter-in-law, Michelle, is holding my book "*Blood in the Streets*" and my oldest son, Chris, is standing behind her flanked by some of my YWAM friends. In the front row is my son, Phillip, and baby Cedar who is being held by my daughter, Cathy.

I've written and published six books, but "*Blood in the Streets: Concealed Carry and the OK Corral*" is by far my best seller.

(Photo courtesy of Jennifer Gibson)

Here I am with my two-year-old son, Cedar, speaking to law-makers at a public meeting at the State Capitol in Lansing, Michigan. Cedar has a way of breaking the ice and disarming strangers, allowing my ideas to be better received. It was an informational meeting sponsored by Gun Owners of America designed to bring attention to the growing "open carry" movement. For more information on open carry, go to www.opencarry.org.

Here I am being interviewed by a local TV station before the Hastings, Michigan open carry rally. My family and I got there and saw TV cameras out front. I kicked into public relations overdrive and gave three interviews before even entering the building. When I got inside I was shocked to see the room packed with 50 gun-toting Second Amendment supporters. We had a great time. (My wife, Sara, is holding our son, Cedar, in the right side of the photo.)

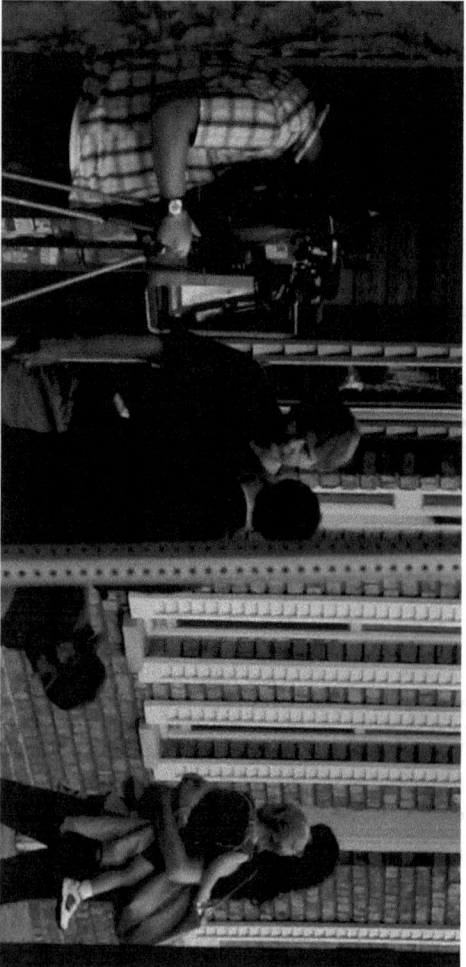

Photo courtesy of Barbara Caris

Photo courtesy of Barbara Caris

This picture shows me marching at an open carry rally in Hastings, Michigan in summer 2008. My friend, Dave Neeson, is in the lead wheelchair toting an antique six-shooter. His grandson, Brock, is pushing him.

I hate the taste of crow. Even with garlic, butter and a few choice herbs and spices; it still doesn't taste like chicken. But on the topic of open carry, I ate some crow, a full helping and then went back for seconds. I had always been adamantly opposed to open carry, but this past summer I helped to organize an open carry march in Hastings, Michigan. I re-evaluated my position and my way of thinking about it. Although I still prefer to carry concealed for personal reasons, I now see the potential value of open carry to the RKBA cause. The people at opencarry.org hold regular open carry events but they do it in a safe and friendly way. (www.opencarry.org)

Here's my 2-year-old son, Cedar, playing with his toy gun. When I was a kid, toy guns were no big deal. Now, because of brain-dead, political correctness, kids get expelled for drawing pictures of toy guns at school. I think kids are smart enough to tell the difference between a real gun and a toy gun. All we have to do is teach them the difference. After all, it's our job; that's what parents do, teach them right from wrong, safe from unsafe, etc. If my 2-year-old son can learn it, then so can your children.

Teach the NRA Eddie Eagle Gun safety Program for kids. When you see a gun: "Stop! Don't touch! Leave the Area! Tell an Adult!" It's so simple a 2-year-old can understand it. So why can't some adults?

(Photo courtesy of Vernon Jenewein)

Midwest Tactical teaches all across Michigan, but our home range is here in Middleville at the home of Dave Stevens, fellow RKBA activist and NRA Instructor. Our basic concealed carry classes have doubled in size since nine-eleven, and now, since the election of Barak Obama, they are growing even larger. We also teach Advanced Tactical classes several times a year. You can check out our course offerings and class schedule at www.mwtac.com.

Last year Midwest Tactical Training partnered with Midwest Training Group (www.midwesttraininggroup.net) to bring Massad Ayoob's Lethal Force Institute to Michigan. It was a huge success and we'll be doing it every year now. Be sure to check our website for class dates and times.

Fourteen

CPL Holders are Different

This is Michigan, and it's been a long, hard, cold winter. But now it's Spring, the sun is out, and the breeze is in my face. I was sitting in the woods today, just reflecting on life, listening to the woodpecker off in the distance, and feeling the gentle sunshine on my face, and it suddenly occurred to me, "Skip, you're different than most people."

I was just reflecting on my life, all I've said and done, all the many things that have happened to me, and I had to admit: I am a different man than most people. Not better, not worse, just different. Some would say, even strange.

How am I different? That's difficult to articulate, because I've been this way my whole life. I just know that people look at my life, or listen to me tell about it, and they get this horrified look in their eyes like I've just grown a second head. I just seem to take my nonconformance for granted, and it didn't hit me until I asked myself this question: "What would you think about someone you met who was just like you?"

Case in point, I was once in Sunday School class, and I heard a man say: "I've had five kids from three different wives, and I'm 48 years old and still having children when most of my friends are becoming grandparents."

And the most terrifying part was - the man's voice was my own.

I didn't quite know what to think about that. Am I crazy? Am I nuts? Nope. I'm just different.

I've made a lot of mistakes; that's for sure and I would be a fool to deny it. There are many things I've done that I would be loath to do again, and many things that have happened to me that I wouldn't wish on my enemies. But one thing is for certain, I've always tried to keep a good attitude, no matter what the situation, and I've always tried to accentuate the positive. In keeping with that personal survival policy, I've become very adept at converting manure into fertilizer.

I suppose there's no intrinsic harm in being different, but I've noticed over the years that there's a price to pay for nonconformance. Some people look at me, see that I'm different, and it scares them. So by now you must be asking yourself: "What does this have to do with the Right to Keep and Bear Arms?"

Well, now, that's a good question, and I have the answer for you. It's quite simple really. Chances are, if you're reading this article, then you're different too. If you're a member of MCRGO, the NRA or Ted Nugent United Sportsmen of America, then you have a certain bent to your personality. You are not content to stick your head in the sand and let the wolves walk by unmolested, free to rape, pillage and plunder with impunity. This puts you in the minority.

But I don't conform. I'm different. And so are you. At one point in your life, you made the active decision to take the road less traveled, to distinguish yourself from the other sheep, to take responsibility for your life and the lives of the ones you love. Now, that's not saying that the other parents, the rest of the flock are poor parents, that they don't love their families, because that's not true at all. They are good parents; they are good little sheep. And there's nothing wrong with that, assuming of course you are willing to accept the consequences of your decision to not arm yourself and protect your family. In my book *Blood in the Streets: Concealed Carry and the OK Corral* I make the following statement:

> "Sheep are born and bred for one purpose: to be killed and to have their parts processed into something useful by predators. They stand on the hill and go "Baa", as they're being slaughtered."

Remember the lesson of Colonel Dave Grossman who constantly tells us that there are three kinds of people: sheep, sheepdogs and wolves. We all know who the wolves are; they are in and out of prison all the time. They take drugs, drink too much, and are prone to cruelty and acts of violence. And we all know who the sheepdogs are: that's you and I, the military, and law enforcement. Every one of us who straps on a sidearm for the purpose of protecting the innocent in society at peril to ourselves, is a sheepdog and a hero. We carry a gun because we love people. Isn't it paradoxical that we are willing to kill people because we love people?

But there are not enough of us. The wolves are too numerous; they are among the flock, and us sheepdogs are spread too thin. We need help.

I have good news: "Help is on the way." More and more often society is starting to accept us. Less and less people look at us like anomalies and more and more like the protectors we are. I suppose it's natural that a sheep is terrified of all fangs. Their terror is understandable because they are defenseless against all sharp teeth. They are unable to distinguish the difference between a gun that would hurt them and a gun that would save them.

But that analogy only goes so far. They may have the personalities and demeanor of sheep, but they are also reasoning human beings with the capacity for rational thought. I believe it's time to raise the bar for all sheep. Anyone who keeps an open mind and takes the time to look at us closely will eventually see that we are not wolves. We can help them and speed the process along by always showing them our best side. We are different than the sheep and the wolf. We have the ability to kill and love at the same time. In fact, ironically enough, sheepdogs kill because they love; it is a total act of unselfishness. On the other hand, wolves kill out of hatred and selfish ambition.

The comparison between CPL holders and average citizens is a stark and profound contrast. But I encourage all of you to get better at articulating why you carry a firearm, because some of us are scaring the hell out of the sheep. Let people get to know your softer side. You are ambassadors, and everything you do reflects on CPL holders everywhere. Take time to reassure the sheep.

Their fears may be irrational and misplaced, but they are still real. Always remember to articulate that you carry a firearm to protect and serve the sheep. It will calm the flock.

The Story Behind the Story

The primary thing that makes concealed carry holders different is their ability to kill and love simultaneously. Perhaps Lt. Colonel David Grossman said it best in his book *"On Killing"*:

"... if you have a capacity for violence, and a deep love for your fellow citizens? What do you have then? A sheepdog, a warrior, someone who is walking the hero's path. Someone who can walk into the heart of darkness, into the universal human phobia, and walk out unscathed."

This seems like an awful paradox, and of course it is. But it makes sense. We just think differently than most people. When faced with possible death, most tremble in fear and paralysis - we act. When others run - we stand. Though we feel love for our fellow man, we kill nonetheless. That confuses the sheep, and I suppose that makes sense too. They're not like us. We're different. I wish we had more different people. We could use the help. Too many wolves - just not enough sheepdogs.

Fifteen

Just in Case

As a general rule, I don't much like politics, especially nowadays. Just talking about it makes my stomach hurt. To listen to the news and the polls, you'd think John McCain and Sarah Palin would have packed it all in and gone home by now. Why are they wasting their time and money when Obama has the election already in the bag? Or so say the pundits. And they're never wrong – except, of course, when they're not right.

Most of my friends and acquaintances are pro-gun conservatives, and I'm hearing some really weird statements right about now. These people, normally level-headed and not prone to over-reaction, are making comments like:

"If Obama wins there's going to be a civil war! The American people will never stand for this!"

On the other hand I've heard:

"If McCain wins there's going to be riots and looting and

martial law!"

Hmmm, seems to me like we lose no matter who wins.

I'm going to make some people mad here, but I have to be honest with my Republican friends. I was disappointed when John McCain won the nomination. I was hoping for a candidate with more conservative roots. It was nothing personal. He's got a lot of good, solid character. I mean he's a war hero for crying out loud! But Senators have just never impressed me much as Presidential candidates. I'm reminded of the Bob Dole campaign. He was a war hero too. But I have to be candid here. Bob Dole had all the charisma of an aging Brook Trout. And from watching the Presidential debates, what I could stand of it, John McCain seems like Bob Dole's twin brother.

Having said that, I'll be voting for Senator Brook Trout simply because I don't trust Obama with my firearms. Despite that, there's a sinking feeling in my gut telling me to stock up on ammo, food, and other supplies, just in case my Chicken Little friends are right and the sky really is falling. And it's not just the election, look at the self-destructing economy as well; look at the state of the world; look at all the natural disasters we've had lately. Is the world on the verge of something really big?

I'm 51 years old, and I've learned not to over-react lightly, but, still . . . Something just hasn't felt right lately. While researching for one of my novels, I ran across a survivalist organization called Ark II. They are committed and fully prepared for the Apocalypse. I get their newsletter every few weeks and they have built a fallout shelter the size of Rhode Island, and stocked it with enough provisions to start a Brave New World. Is it really that bad? Is America on its last leg? It reminds me of that Brendan Fraser movie *"Blast from the Past"*.

But I can tell you that confidence overall in American civilization seems to be plummeting. I used to teach only one concealed carry class a month, but now I travel all over the place barely getting a weekend off to hunt and fish and be with my family. Sure, the money's great, and I can't really complain. At every concealed carry class I ask people why they're getting their permits and more and more I'm getting one of two answers:

1. It's the rise in crime. I don't feel safe anymore.

2. It's the elections. I have to get my carry permit before they pass a law against it.

A few days ago someone sent me an email stating that President Bush had formed a task force whose sole purpose was to come up with plans and procedures for declaring martial law should riots occur after the elections or should the economy totally collapse and the law of the jungle take over. At first I filed it with the email I got from the lawyer in Kenya offering me 20 million dollars to help a young widow regain her husband's estate because of some legal technicality. Honestly, the things some people will do to part me from my money. At first I disregarded it, but then, the more I thought about it, the more I thought about it. And then I thought about it some more, and some more, and some more. By then I was obsessing. The paranoid part of me wanted to run out and buy an assault rifle, 10,000 rounds of ammo, and build my own fallout shelter.

Finally, I put on the brakes and got hold of myself. It can't be this bad. I was reminded of some of my Christian friends who are convinced that Jesus is coming next Thursday at 5PM. Will he? Probably not. Could he? Maybe. But then again, people have been warning about his second coming since the day he left about 2,000 years ago. But then I compared today's survivalist scenario with the second coming of Christ. It went kind of like this:

I'm not walking around wearing a sandwich sign all day that says "Repent, the end of the age is near!" I would look like a fool! On the other hand, spiritually, I do believe that Jesus will come again and I try to prepare my soul on a daily basis – just in case.

And, suddenly, it all made sense to me. I don't need to start burying survival barrels out back or dig a fallout shelter, but there are many things I can do that aren't so extreme. Truth be known, I have been stocking up on ammo, reloading supplies, canned goods, and looking into alternative ways to heat my house. We've even saved up a chunk of money – just in case. (And no, it's not buried in a barrel out back. The last thing I need is some fool digging around in my back yard.)

I've always had a self-sufficient mindset; always planted a garden; always hunted my own meat; always learned how to protect myself and my family– just in case. And it's always felt good to be prepared. I think a lot of CPL holders are like that too. We see a potential threat and then we prepare for it as best we can.

But I want to caution all of you against going too far and then looking like a complete idiot. It's never as bad as it seems. Well, except for the times, when it's worse than it seems. Hmmm, I'm reminded of a man named Noah who lived long ago. He built an ark in the desert and all his friends laughed – until it rained, and rained, and rained. Then they weren't laughing anymore; they were too busy dog paddling.

I guess what I'm saying is this. Building a full-blown ark is probably overkill, but could it really hurt anything to have a rubber raft or a dingy in your garage? I for one don't think so. Hope for the best – prepare for the worst. Just in case.

The Story Behind the Story

I wrote this column for Michigan Coalition for Responsible Gun Owners (MCRGO) about 2 weeks before the Presidential election. It seems to me that it's getting harder and harder for a true conservative to pull the lever. I was never excited about John McCain, even though I liked him as a person. But when you compare John McCain to Barak Obama, the task gets easier.

Today it's November 7th, three days after Barak Obama was elected President, and I can't help but wonder: will he govern from the far left or from the center? If he governs in accordance with his liberal voting record, then he'll be prying a pistol from my cold, dead fingers.

My gut tells me he won't. He's too smart for that and he'll want a second term. So he'll govern from the center, giving just enough to his liberal friends in Congress to keep them from picking the flesh from his political carcass.

In a way, it's rather exciting: the economy is going south, terrorists are closing in, crime is rampant, illegal aliens are coming up from the border fast! Okay, so exciting may be a bit optimistic. But I've always been a real glass half-full kind of guy.

By the time you read this book, Obama will be sworn in along with the new Congress and we should know our fate for the next four years to come. Some of my conservative friends are sharpening their bayonets and stocking up on ammo in anticipation for the apocalypse. I'll hold off for a little while longer. Things are seldom as bad as they seem - except of course, when they're worse than they seem.

And now please bow your heads so we can all pray. I hate politics.

Sixteen

Charlton Heston 1923 to 2008 - A Tribute

This afternoon, when I heard that Charlton Heston had died, I was surprised at the depth of my own sadness. We had never met, indeed, I had never even seen him except through the aid of television and the silver screen. But one thing is undeniable: the man left his mark. Mr. Heston was always larger than life to me, instilling a sense of awe even through the limiting filter of a television's screen. Let's face it, the man was Moses, and in my eyes, he carried all the power and prestige of the ten commandments. I was just a child when I first saw him play Moses and Ben Hur, so it was only natural that he appeared even bigger than life to me. In my little boy's eyes, Mr. Heston really could part the Red Sea or send forth a series of plagues upon an obstinate Pharaoh, bringing the leader of Egypt to his knees.

Later, as a teenager, I saw him in *Planet of the Apes* and remember enjoying him immensely and being shocked at the end of the movie when he found the Stature of Liberty jutting up through the sand. Now, as I look back, I associate the movie *Planet of the Apes* with our own twisted and decadent society, realizing that so much in life has been turned around; it's almost as if the monkeys are in charge now. We are indeed backwards: North has become South, and South has become North.

Then, as an adult, I didn't think too often about Mr. Heston, other than to view his movies once in a while, usually late at night or on the weekend. But then in 1998, something very special happened. He became my President. No, not President of the United States, but President of the National Rifle Association. I can still recall his profound words: "From my cold, dead, hands!" For me, and for many Americans, Charlton Heston legitimized the National Rifle Association, giving it true worldwide media exposure and prestige, thereby moving it further into the mainstream. Finally, someone from Hollywood was standing up for sanity and reason and the United States Constitution.

I didn't know Charlton Heston personally, so I spoke with someone who did, and this is what he told me about him.

"I was privileged to have the legendary Charlton Heston on my radio show in Detroit back in 1995, and there, as during many such memorable encounters as a fellow NRA Board of Director and NRA President, he was everything the legend indicated him to be, and more. He defined intellect, humor, goodwill, decency, American spirit and dignity. As both awe-inspiring actor, civil rights leader and US Constitutional activist, he lived the ultimate "we the people" participation and celebration. His unwavering fight for Second Amendment rights proved a courage unrivaled in the oftentimes unforgiving, fickle Hollywood industry, and he deeply inspired me and legions of freedom-loving Americans to always stand up for the self-evident-truth-fueled American Dream. Mr. Heston and his warrior spirit lives on in the hearts and souls of freedom fighters everywhere."

-- Ted Nugent --

No, I didn't know him personally, but I do know him through his work, and his work inspires me to become a better person, to live my life to a higher standard and to search my soul for the right thing to do, and then to carry through with it. I wish I had known him more, but that was not possible. His movies will have to do.

In my latest book *Laughter and Tears: Living both Sides of Life* I wrote an essay about Mr. Heston's generation in which I say:

"My grandmother was one of the greatest influences on my young life. She taught me to cook from scratch; she led me to Jesus; she told me about the depression, growing up in the muck fields, and the Second World War. She's dead now, and I shudder to think what will happen when all the old people are gone. Old people are the heart and soul of our nation; the conscience of America; the disappearing link of common sense and logic. What will happen when they're gone? What will become of us and our children? Who will pass on our history and humanity to the next generation"

Mr. Heston exemplified our greatest generation.

I believe that the world doesn't exist for the individual, but that the individual exists for the world. To find the meaning in life, you must first find something greater than yourself to serve. Through service to others, life is given meaning. Charlton Heston's life was given meaning and purpose and lives on, not by virtue of his celebrity status, because that will fade with his earthly passing, but because of his lifelong service to God – Family – and Country.

Now that Mr. Heston has moved on to the next life, I can't help but feel he's looking down at us now, still holding that famous flintlock over his head and shouting down to the anti-gunners "My hands are dead and cold, and you never got my gun!" He stood up for what he believed in. He lived a consistent life. He was a servant. He was a leader. Charlton Heston made his mark.

And now, it's up to us as we carry on without him, to guard that torch of freedom, defending it with our lives and all we hold dear, making sure that no one ever rides up on the beach and sees the Statue of Liberty buried in the sand. I for one, will always remember Mr. Heston and follow his lead. Let us all raise that torch of freedom high above our heads and cry out with one, loud voice, "*From my cold, dead hands!*"

The Story Behind the Story

Charlton Heston was born on October 4th, 1923 as John Charles Carter in No Man's Land, a disputed unincorporated area on the shore of Lake Michigan between the Chicago suburbs of Evanston and Wilmette, Illinois. He died from pneumonia on April 5th, 2008 after a long and productive life.

Charlton Heston was my hero, and they don't make them like him anymore. You know you're getting old when your heroes begin to die. One by one, they fall and pass from everyday life: John Wayne (June 11th, 1979), Jimmy Stewart (July 2nd, 1997), Ronald Reagan (June 5th, 2004), Rosa Parks (October 24, 2005), Charlton Heston (April 5th, 2008), and the list goes on; it keeps getting bigger.

We are not the sum total of the people we respect, but the people we admire are a great reflection on who we really are, in the inner recesses of our soul, in the night, when no one else can see us, we are a glimpse of the ones we call hero.

Charlton Heston was one of those heroes. He was the latest in a long line of heroes to fall. He affected my life forever. He stood up. He made his mark. He lives on through the courage and service of those he inspired. Thank you Mr. Heston. God bless you.

Seventeen

Just Normal Folk

Sometimes when I write my articles I have to hide. That's what I'm doing now. I'm out in my driveway, in the Monte Carlo, typing away on my laptop. There are times when it's the only way I can write. You see, I still have three kids at home. This morning, I spent an hour with my two-year-old son. We made a tent from a bed sheet by draping it over the book case and then anchoring the corners with toys. It was an engineering wonder, so far as toddlers are concerned. Then, while inside the makeshift tent, I watched as my son, Cedar, proceeded to take every single book off the shelf and stack it on the floor beside us. Most of the books belong to his mother. There were books on Quantum physics, electrical engineering, and even on fuel cell technology. But all Cedar kept saying was "This is my book! This is my book!" and then he would stack it into a random pile.

Forty five minutes later, after my wife finished her elliptical machine workout, she ventured upstairs and saw us playing inside the tent. I don't know what she was thinking, but I do know what she said "Those are MY books! They're worth a lot of money! Who's going to clean up this mess?" Cedar toddled off on other two-year old missions, leaving me to face the music and clean up the mess.

This afternoon, we'll be going to a soccer game. It's my 12-year-old son, Phillip's, first game of the season. We'll watch and cheer and perhaps even tell the referee he's blind. Then afterwards, we'll go out for fast food to either celebrate the victory or to console the heart of a young boy who just got his butt kicked. It's a normal day.

Then, tomorrow, we'll go to church. I'll wear blue jeans, my NRA tactical vest, and I'll be sporting a Smith and Wesson MP 9mm within my Tucker Gun Leather Inside the Waistband holster. We'll sing songs, worship God, give our tithe and listen to the sermon. I like church. It gives me time to think.

Afterwards, we'll go out for dinner, talk about family matters and Sara and I will problem solve and try to plan for the coming week. While we're doing this, we'll be holding on to a squirming toddler and answering adolescent questions like "Do you think this chicken cares that I'm eating it?" or "Dad, what kind of car do you think I'll drive when I'm old?" And all the while the toddler is screaming "Potty! Potty!" It's just a normal day.

So here I am halfway through my article and you still don't know my point. How can this possibly relate to personal defense and the Second Amendment? Have you lost your mind, Skip? What are you driving at? Okay, here's my point. For decades, the media has pounded it into the heads of the general public that gun owners are aggressive, unsophisticated, fanatical, and even bloodthirsty. But you and I know the truth. However, it's not enough to simply KNOW the truth. You must also help to SPREAD the truth.

We know that when a lie goes unanswered, it doesn't necessarily become the truth, but it will eventually be believed by more and more people. These things have a way of self-fulfilling the prophecy. Remember the words of Joseph Goebbels the Minister of Propaganda for the Nazi regime? *If you tell a lie long enough, it becomes the truth.*

In my opinion, us firearm owners have room for improvement here. We have a moral obligation to fight against the lies by telling the truth. We are not gun-toting rednecks hell-bent on shooting someone. Rather, we are sophisticated and educated. More importantly, we are families. We are mothers; we are fathers; we are doctors; we are factory workers; we are college students; we are clerks, dentists, lawyers; we are police officers; we are simply Americans who own firearms for hunting, recreation and to protect our families.

This past week I was impressed with Alaska Governor Sarah Palin. In fact, much of the Republican Convention was a focus on feelings. I think they've finally figured out that many people don't like politicians, especially swing voters. Regardless of your party of choice, you have to admit that the video biographies of Sarah Palin, Cindy McCain, and John McCain, were emotional masterpieces. People don't want to vote for a "politician". They want to vote for a genuine person. And Sarah Palin appears to be a "real" person, with a husband and kids and feelings and she hunts and shoots and even rides a Harley!

Is all of it true? I don't know. I suppose if she's elected, then we'll find out who she is.

But that's not my point. My point is we are all walking, talking, video biographies. We're not stereotypes yet we've allowed the media to place us in a box labeled "Bad American". I say it's time to fight back, but not with guns and not with anger. Anger will not serve us in this cause.

Instead, talk to your anti-gun neighbor. Smile and tell them about your family. They vote just like you do. You can win more votes by talking about church and family than about caliber and carry methods. Go out of your way to talk to antigunners. But don't preach to them and stay away from politics.

Also, I am learning, that the Republican party no longer has a monopoly on the Second Amendment. This past Spring I taught an MCRGO-sponsored CPL class to 45 State Representatives and their staff. Over half of them were Democrats. None of them had two heads or even a third eyeball. I was amazed at how "human" they appeared. In fact, I became friends with many of them, and I enjoyed their company. When out on the range shooting guns, there is no "party", just Americans out there having fun throwing lead.

So here is my challenge to you. Lighten up. Show people who you really are. Talk to the antigunners about your family and your feelings. Show them the truth: that us gun toters are really just people who carry firearms to protect the friends and family we love. Become the friends of antigunners as well. Only then can you turn them from the dark side of gun control politics and usher them into the light of self defense.

The Story Behind the Story

This article ran in the MCRGO Newsletter shortly after the Republican National Convention of 2008. But very little of it is about politics. Instead, it's about family; it's about normalcy; it's about personal protection, the media bias, and the jaded view of gun ownership in America. My blood boils when I think of the media and the duty they have neglected and abused. They have a constitutional responsibility to turn on the light of truth, to reveal lies and to keep politicians honest. They no longer do that, and now our country is lesser because of it.

We have allowed ourselves to be painted as gun-toting, blood thirsty maniacs, running around with deadly weapons, waiting for the first opportunity to shoot someone. We didn't earn the reputation, but neither have we effectively fought against it. We have to do better. And that's what I was thinking when I wrote this article. We have to do better. We can do better. We have to tell the truth because no one else will. We have to show the world who we really are. In this article, I show the world who I am at the very core of my being. And I urge all of you now to do the same. Become vulnerable. Show your neighbor who you are. The world will be a better place because of it.

Eighteen

Reach Down and Grab some Scrote!

I just finished reading an article on the rise of crime here in Michigan, most notably armed robberies and bank robberies. One major city reported these types of crimes had doubled compared to the first quarter of last year, while another city's armed crime had tripled. The focus of the article was "Why is this happening?"

Usually, when I read an article like this in the mainstream press, it is obvious to me that the reporter's opinions are a foregone conclusion: "Guns are the problem. There are too many; they are too easy to get; they must be further restricted."

But this article (from a fairly liberal publication) both surprised and encouraged me. The reporter spent a minimal amount of time on guns, and focused more on the criminal. That is, the person who actually commits the crime instead of blaming his tool of choice. The reporter talked about how we've desensitized our young people with violent video games and movies, how young criminals are becoming more and more brutal and inhumane in their crimes. (That doesn't surprise me. Didn't he get the memo from Lt. Colonel David Grossman, author of *"Why are we Teaching our Children to Kill?"*)

Excuse me folks, but this confuses me. Call me simple and daft, but if young people are becoming more and more violent, due to desensitization via video games and movies, then, hmmm, dare I say it? Why can't the parents just turn off the TV, unplug the Game Cube, and put a book in the little boy's hands? Is that too simple?

But I can hear parents groaning all across the state at my ridiculous suggestion. "What! Take away the TV? Take away the video games? I can't do that!" My simple reply is: "Why not?" You're the parents aren't you? You are the ones in charge – right?

Well, maybe it's not so simple. After all, over half our families have only one parent or are blended families. It's tough Skip! It's not easy raising kids these days. Look at all the drugs, all the promiscuity, all the disrespect! We can't be blamed for that!

Oh really? Why not? I'll ask the question again: "You are the ones in charge aren't you?"

Perhaps we've hit on something here. Maybe the parents aren't in charge anymore? Maybe they've handed the keys of the family asylum over to the lunatics. Now, don't get me wrong, kids aren't lunatics. But, on the other hand, they sure as hell aren't qualified to be running their own lives.

Let me interject an important parenting tip here: "Children are usurpers of all authority left unattended."

Kids want boundaries; they want limits. They need them, and when they don't get them, they'll keep breaking rules until someone strong enough steps in and takes the keys away from them. You ask me "Why"? Why do kids want us to take control of their lives? That's simple. They want us to take control because deep down, in their heart of hearts, when they lie awake at night struggling with puberty, the opposite sex, peer pressure, and the meaning of life, in their heart of hearts; they know they're not qualified to make life-changing decisions; they know that when push comes to shove, when the rubber meets the road, deep down inside they know that despite all their blustering, whining and complaining and screaming for control; they know that they're just ignorant kids who don't know their butts from a hole in the ground.

And that's why all you parents have to take control of your kids. They're counting on you to do it, to be strong, to seize possession of the remote control that runs their lives and to give them healthy boundaries and limits.

But you say "Skip, you don't understand how tough it is to raise kids all by yourself. My spouse left me 5 years ago, and I've got two jobs just to make ends meet. I can't do it on my own! You're being naïve and insensitive!"

Oh my. There's that word again - "insensitive". I'm being naïve? I think not. I was the custodial father of a 4-year-old boy and a 6-year-old girl for several years before I remarried. I was forced to hold down three jobs just to pay the bills and put food on the table. Was it tough? You're damned straight it was tough! It was nearly impossible! But nearly impossible is different than totally impossible. Almost every day I would come home, dragging my butt to the sitter's house, pick up my kids, then get that second burst of wind and energy long enough to play with them. Sometimes I would fall asleep on the couch while they sat on my stomach playing games like "Doctor Daddy" or "Daddy Beautician". More than once I went to bed with make-up on my face and bobby pins in my hair, too exhausted to clean myself off. (My daughter loved those games and she still talks about them many years later.)

But I'm going to be blunt here, folks, and I feel I've earned the right, since I've been in your single-parent shoes. I know it's tough, but you need to reach down and pull yourself up by your own scrotum (you women too) because that's what it takes nowadays to be a good parent. You need courage, and most of all resiliency. You need that indomitable, indefatigable personality that says "I'll never give up and I'll never give in!" The enemy is all around us folks, and they're pressing in on every side. These days you have to be part parent and part Marine to get the job done right.

Yes, I know it's tough, but it's not impossible, and your responsibility has never been greater. Guns don't cause crime, it's parents who can't say no. Telling your kids "No" quite possibly could be the most loving thing you ever do as a parent. Teach them boundaries; teach them respect for themselves and others; teach them "no"; teach them the irrefutable natural law of cause and effect. If you break my rules, I will be there to hold you accountable.

I am your parent. I love you. I will do the job. I am here for you, even if you kick and scream and push me away.

I recently read another news article about parents who ask police departments to come into their homes and search their children's bedrooms for drugs and guns. Excuse me? Reality check here! Hey people! You're the parent! You're the mom! You're the dad! Get your cowardly, lazy butt in there and search the room yourself! And if you find drugs or guns, then deal with it! Our families are the most precious asset America has. For God's sake don't outsource raising your own children! Especially to the government! They can't even balance their own checkbooks, so what makes you think politicians can resolve complicated family matters. It's none of their business! Your children belong to you! That's why they're called "your children" and not "wards of the state"!

The causes of crime are complicated and multi-faceted. So what! Part of the problem is kids without boundaries, kids who don't value human life, kids who are mean and mad as hell.

Riddle me this Batman. "Why are so many kids angry and mean?"

Answer: Because deep down inside they believe that if you really loved them, if you really cared, you would step up, take charge, and give them the mother of all Gameboy enemas!

So now, reach down, grab some scrote and do the job you signed on for. Be the man! Be the woman! Be the parent! Teach your kids how to be human! No one can do it as well as a parent.

The Story Behind the Story

I remember writing that commentary and I took a lot of flak for it. I made a few parents downright furious! At the time it bothered me that I'd offended people, but after reading it just now, several months later, I still stand behind my writing. Primarily, because it's true. Kids without boundaries grow up to become muggers, rapists, and bank robbers.

It was pointed out to me that it would have been better received if I'd used words that were less harsh. I don't think so. They didn't like the message, so they shot the messenger. The people who complained in their angry emails were the ones most in need of courage.

One man wrote me the following email:

"I just read your article "Reach Down and Grab some Scrote!". "What a bunch of bunk". Wake-up, smell the coffee. All that you are preaching may have been effective 20 years ago, but the powers have changed. Today the children are in power. If you took away a child's TV today, the child could/would merely report it to any School personnel, or be overheard talking to a friend about it, by School personnel. The School personnel are required under penalty of law, to report the issue to the over zealous Child Protective Services, who in turn will investigate the issue and if found true, will prosecute for neglect and/or abuse."

This man has become afraid of his own children. What a sad picture of America. Is there any hope?

Another man complained about my use of the word "scrotum" and "enema". He was deeply offended. I asked a friend of mine, the king of off-color and double-en tend re if people were still really that sensitive and pristine about slang? Ted Nugent answered me like this:

"Hell Yeah! Some people are incredibly unsophisticated. 60+% of them wouldn't get Letterman or Leno humor IF they stayed up late enough to see/hear it!! Dear God!! they still think WANG DANG SWEET POOTANG is vulgar!! Hammeron!!"

Yep. That's my Ted. I suppose a little bit of criticism is good, whether it's valid or irrational. I've learned to take it all in, analyze it, keep what is good and discard the rest. Writers need a very thick skin. Sometimes us authors just have to reach down and grab some ... well, you get the idea.

Nineteen

Sheep in Shepherd's Clothing

I heard the shot that killed me and that confused me, because in the Marine Corps I was always told that you never hear the bullet that gets you, the logic being, so long as you hear the gunshot, then you're going to be okay. But I wasn't okay. I knew that much for sure. But I'm getting ahead of myself, so let me start from the beginning.

I was in one of those pistol-free zones again, the ones I hate so much. This time it was a church Bible study. My wife was with me, and the study was just getting ready to end. Sara grabbed her coat and we both got up discreetly to leave while the others had closing prayer. People always stand around and talk afterwards and it was late, so we wanted to get back home in time for our two-year-old son's bedtime. I've always loved my children's bedtime routine, especially while they're little. I fix his bottle, while my wife changes his diaper, brushes his teeth and puts him in his pajamas. Then I meet them upstairs as she is laying him down in bed. I place my hand on his forehead and pray for him: "Dear God, please be with Cedar tonight. Watch over him, protect him and keep him safe. Help him to sleep good and have happy dreams. Amen." It's cute the way he closes his eyes while I pray for him. Then he says "Mommy pray." Sara does the same, and then he says "Hug". We both hug and kiss him, say good night and the lights go out. It is the best part of my day. So I am always eager to put him in bed and I am loath to miss his bedtime. But now I digress.

We rushed quietly out of the Bible study and into the hallway. My wife put on her coat, and I looked around for my own. It wasn't there! It was then I noticed that the black, metal lock on the church poor box was broken as if it had been tampered with. I looked over at it, sat down on the bench and placed my head down into my hands with my elbows on my knees. I looked down at the floor and said, "Honey, do you think someone stole my coat?"

I didn't hear or see the man walk up. I just felt the muzzle of his pistol press against the top of my forehead. I didn't move. I knew I should, but I couldn't. I was paralyzed with fear. And then he spoke a short, emotionless and simple reply to my question. He said, "Yeah."

Almost immediately he fired his pistol. I heard the deafening roar and then everything went black and silent. But I heard the explosion, and I remember thinking "I can't be dead. I heard the shot! I must be alive! I can't be dead!" But there was nothing but blackness. I couldn't move. I had the powers of rational thought, but I couldn't hear anything, see anything or feel anything. I couldn't even smell the gun smoke. Things that should have been there were missing from the picture. All this happened within a matter of seconds and then my first response was: "I've been shot. My wife is next. But I don't hear anything. I can't move! I can't protect my wife. I love her. I can't move! I can't stop this guy from killing her!"

And then my eyes opened and I woke up from my dream. I looked over to my right and there was my wife in bed sleeping soundly and safely. The clock said 7AM. I closed my eyes again and tried to get back to sleep, but it wouldn't work. I got up and started to get ready for church, but no matter how hard I tried, I couldn't quite shake the myriad of thoughts and feelings bumping into each other inside of me. The dream had really shaken me up.

I've heard it said, that if you die in your dream, then you die in real life. Now I know that to be false. But for many years I believed it. Several times I've had a dream of falling off a cliff, but I would always wake up just before hitting the ground. I find it more than coincidence that I had this dream just a few hours before going to church in a pistol-free zone.

I thought about it for a while, and my fear gradually gave way to anger. After all, anger is almost always a secondary emotion. Pistol-free zones do that to me every time. What kind of a world is it where sheep are allowed to disarm the shepherds? I have always had that warrior-protector instinct inside me, even as a child. Even though I was a small boy, I never rolled over and let the playground bully have his way. I always fought back. I suppose that's why I was drawn to the Marine Corps, and then, later in life, why I was drawn to Ted Nugent, the NRA and MCRGO. To deny my warrior instinct would be to deny my own soul. I have a need to protect the people I love, but a small handful of politically savvy sheep have disarmed me.

I think one of the biggest complaints that CPL holders have is the pistol-free zones, but really, who is to blame for that? How can we blame the sheep; they're just acting on their instincts? We're the sheepdogs. We're the ones with dominant personalities. Shouldn't we be working to put the sheep in their place? Shouldn't we be herding them instead of them herding us? The answer of course is an undeniable and resounding YES! So what has happened? Why is everything backwards? How is it that a handful of sheep have been allowed to masquerade and take control, to become sheep in shepherd's clothing?

The answer is simple: the shepherds have become lazy, and political sheep are usurpers of all power left unattended. There are over 160,000 CPL holders in Michigan. How many of us are active NRA members and MCRGO members? Answer: Not enough! In fact, it has always been true that 10 percent of the people do 90 percent of the work. Actually, if the truth be known, when it comes to pro-Second Amendment workers, this statement is more true: "5 percent of the people do 95 percent of the work.

To those of you who are members, who are working hard, and never giving up, I salute you! Godspeed and carry on! But the rest of you, the 95 percent who haven't joined MCRGO or the NRA, those who lay around complaining about pistol-free zones but never doing anything to change the law, I have no sympathy for you. In fact, you are not very good shepherds at all. You have given up your staff and aren't guarding the flock and its freedom the way you should. You are the shameless slackers and it's time you carried your weight. It's time for all of you to pick up your staff and follow the rest of us.

I don't suppose this will be a very popular commentary, but that's my opinion and that's how I see it. Sometimes a sheepdog, even a good one, just gets sick and tired of working overtime while so many others sit around and do nothing. If the shoe fits, wear it. Get off your butts! Join the NRA! Join MCRGO! Take away my nightmares!

Note: to join Michigan Coalition for Responsible Gun Owners, go to www.mcrgo.org. You have no excuse. We now have a special "Friends of MCRGO" membership for only $15. Contact me at skipcoryell@hotmail.com for more details. You can also join the National Rifle Association with a special "Liberty" membership for only $10 by going to www.nra.org.

The Story Behind the Story

I wrote this article during a transitional time in my life. We had been living in Iowa for all of 2007, but then we moved back to my lifelong home of Michigan. One of the nice things about Iowa, was that pistol-free zones were few and far between. I liked that.

But we had just moved back to Michigan where one of the pistol-free zones is church. Because we'd moved into a new neighborhood, we went to a new place of worship, where people didn't know me. (My old Michigan church was an hour's drive and gas was getting very expensive.) I was faced with a dilemma: The Michigan statute says that I can't carry in a church without the permission of the presiding official. But the pastor didn't know me. How was I going to find a graceful way to ask a stranger "Hey, do you mind if I carry a gun in here?" Answer: there is no graceful way.

I decided to give it three months, make some friends, and let the people warm up to me before asking. As a result, I had to disarm myself for three months every time I went to church. This really rubbed me the wrong way. In fact, it got so bad that I found it hard to focus on the sermon each Sunday. I was becoming bitter. Finally, I went to the Pastor and explained the situation to him. He said he'd never heard of it before and that he would go to the denomination's home office and ask for the policy.

He never got back to me. Shortly thereafter, we started driving an hour to our old church where I was again allowed to carry. In fact, they asked me to join the church Emergency Response Team, which I did. Now I work to train other CPL holders to protect against a church attack such as the one in Arvada, Colorado (YWAM base) and New Life Community Church in Colorado Springs.

Did I mention that I hate pistol-free zones?

I hate this one most of all. What happened to separation of church and state? It would appear that it is a one-way street, paved and maintained by the government (i.e., the state). Not a good situation. Let's work hard and change this.

Twenty

Open Carry – Is America Ready?

Three years ago I wrote the following in my book titled *Blood in the Streets: Concealed Carry and the OK Corral*:

"I teach my students that there is no advantage to anyone knowing that they are carrying a concealed pistol."

And then later on in the book I said:

"In my very humble opinion, in most scenarios, open carry is a bad decision. Open carry is stupid carry. Concealed carry is smart carry. Keep it hidden. Keep it smart."

For the past 8 years I have consistently taught in my classes that open carry is a very risky proposition, but I am starting to re-evaluate the severity of that opinion. I am always gathering new data, new experiences and new technology and then applying it to my everyday life. I think this is the best way to go, and I'm not so dogmatic as to think that nothing ever changes. Some things change, some things don't.

In my book I describe two reasons why open carry is stupid carry.

1. There is no tactical advantage to open carry.
2. It scares people. Michigan is not ready for open carry.

I believe that the first reason is still valid and probably always will be. Open carry gives away the element of surprise and I don't want to do that. Here's what I wrote in the book, and I still hold to it:

"As a former Marine Infantryman, I understand that the most important asset in a battle is the element of surprise. I know full well that if I can retain that equalizing "surprise element", then I can overcome most other odds, be they superior firepower or superior numbers. If I open carry, that advantage is gone. But if I carry concealed, I have a greater number of options that are open to me. I can wait and see what happens. I can duck behind cover. I can draw my firearm and surprise the bad guys with a hail of deadly gunfire. I can wait for them to make a mistake, then act decisively and with conviction."

However, despite all that, something happened a few days ago which has caused me to re-evaluate my strong stance against open carry. Let me tell you what happened.

A friend of mine came to me, one of my long-time Second Amendment activist buddies, and told me that he was going to walk through downtown main street, daring the Chief of Police to arrest him. My first thought was: this doesn't sound like a good idea. In fact, several years ago I had spoken with the Chief in that town and I knew that he was dead-set against open carry and even against concealed carry. Once, in a private conversation in his office, I asked him what he would do if I were to walk through town wearing a pistol and holster. He told me in no uncertain terms that he would arrest me. I believed him.

So when my friend came to me, I was concerned about his plan. I was convinced that he would be arrested. But then he asked me to join him and I didn't have the heart to tell him no. He was too good a friend and we'd been through the political activist trenches during the concealed carry debate, so we started making plans for the event.

Now you have to understand that I seldom do things small. It's just not in my personality. Besides, if I was going to walk through a city with a pistol strapped to my side, I wanted company. So I told a few friends, and they told their friends and then their friends told their friends – and then it hit the internet – all over the country. When I told Ted Nugent he was all for it and said to put it on tednugent.com, which I did. From there it migrated to other websites and soon I was getting emails from people all across the country.

This two-man event was growing out of control. And then the media started to call.

I figured since I was going to be interviewed by channel 3, channel 8, and the Detroit Free Press, that I might want to know something about open carry before I actually did it. So I emailed the guys at www.opencarry.org and they were very helpful, pointing me to videos of previous open carry events and other news sources. But I have to tell you, that even after I'd educated myself, I was still as nervous as a frog in a blender.

Just to be safe, we contacted the County Prosecutor, the State Police and the State Attorney General, just to make sure that what we were doing was legal. To my surprise, they all agreed that it was. They even pointed me to several legal sources: Attorney General Opinion 7101 on brandishing, and MCL 750.234d. I was reassured, but still nervous. Just to make sure, we recruited an attorney to attend our event, just in case.

All this happened in the span of four days, and on the night before, I didn't get to sleep until 4:30 AM. I emailed Ted Nugent for moral support and asked his advice. He emailed back in typical Tedlike fashion:

"YOU are in charge!! Carry on! Sincerity delivers the day. Godspeed"

Quite frankly, that's what he always says. Be sincere! Speak from the heart! Take control! He's such an alpha male. I secretly wished that he could fly on up and walk with me on this thing, but he had some lame excuse about a concert tour in Canada.

So I went to the event the next day with my wife and three kids. On the way there I called Dave and asked him how many people had come. He said he was still there alone. That was less than a half hour before the event. It was then I began to curse myself for being stupid enough to think that others would put themselves at risk alongside me. To top it all off, the kids were fighting with each other in the car and my nerves were tighter than a gnat's butt stretched over a barrel.

We got there and I saw TV cameras out front. I kicked into public relations activist overdrive and gave three interviews before even entering the building. When I got inside I was shocked to see the room was packed with about 50 Second Amendment supporters. Some of them I knew, others I didn't. But it was good to see them all. They were my backup.

I talked to the troops, telling them to keep smiling, say good things, and to not touch their firearms no matter what. Number one rule: 1. Pistols never clear leather. Number two rule: 2. Be nice, smile, live the golden rule.

Larry came up and told me that there was a group of anti's who might give us trouble. I thought to myself, *Great! Just what we need. Idiots bent on making us look bad!* I told everyone not to talk to them, just let them make fools of themselves. Any altercation would undoubtedly be blamed on us and defeat our mission which was to educate the public that open carry was both legal and constitutional and that gun owners need not be feared by the general population.

We walked outside, the cameras following our every move. We walked down 2 blocks to city hall. Shopkeepers came out of their stores to watch, and people on the street took pictures with their cell phones.

A strange thing happened to me. I was no longer nervous. In fact, I was downright happy, gleeful even. It felt good to no longer have to hide my pistol behind a shirt. At that moment, while walking down main street with all eyes watching, I felt more like a free man than at any other point in my life.

We walked two blocks back to the county courthouse and gathered at the veteran's memorial in front of the fountain. I told them the story of how Dave and I had crashed our first County Gun Board meeting back in 1999, subsequently opening it up to the public. Then I gave a 5-minute speech. The Detroit Free Press called it a red-meat speech, but I'm not even sure what that means. Here's a small excerpt:

> "We have been given a birthright of freedom, and that birthright was passed on to each one of us from our father and our father's father and his father before him. The right to keep and bear arms, the right to protect our families, the right to ward off the wolves is as old as creation itself. It was infused into our spiritual DNA, into the everlasting consciousness of humanity and it forever runs deep in the race."

I like red meat. Afterwards, people lingered, not wanting the moment to end. An hour later people were still there. Finally, I left, totally exhausted and my spirit fulfilled.

What we had done was risky, but the risk had paid off. Barry County was now open to "open carry". I'm glad we did it.

So, I find myself re-evaluating my stance. Obviously, concealed carry is still the best tactical choice. Nonetheless, I suspect that many in America are ready for more. I believe that open carry, when properly practiced, is a useful tool in educating and desensitizing the public to firearm usage. For decades the anti's have taught that Guns equal crime; therefore, gun owners equal criminals.

That couldn't be further from the truth, and last week in a small town in Michigan, 40 plus gun owners proved it.

The Story Behind the Story

I hate the taste of crow. Even with garlic, butter and a few choice herbs and spices; it still doesn't taste like chicken. But on this one topic, I ate some crow, a full helping and then went back for seconds. I hope I never have to eat it again.

I had always been adamantly opposed to open carry, but something happened in my life that questioned my view. I was forced to re-evaluate and then to modify my position. It seems that all of life is a journey of adaptation and change. Some things change some things don't. The trick is to know the difference between the two.

The above article is the prequel to a three-part series that appeared in the MCRGO newsletter and also on tednugent.com. It was never meant to be a series, but sometimes stories have a mind and will of their own. People liked the first one, so I just kept on going. I hope you enjoy them all, and that they cause you to think and question your views, whether you change them or not.

Twenty-one

The Open Carry Debate – A Sheep's Eye View

This article is part 1 in a 3-part series on the continuing and ever-growing "Open carry" debate. It's been in the news a lot lately, and I suspect the focus on open carry will increase before it subsides, so we need to discuss it. Hopefully, people will keep an open mind, a clear head, and a sincere heart as they continue to form their opinions.

Many of you know that a few weeks ago I held an open carry rally in Hastings, Michigan where over 40 people attended and walked the streets openly carrying their pistols. This was my first experience with open carry and I enjoyed it. As you can imagine, I received a lot of attention from three segments of society that merit conversation: the unarmed public, police officers, and concealed carry holders.

In this commentary I'll be dealing with the unarmed public, who, for all practical purposes are defenseless sheep. In order to understand my opinion on human sheep, and to fully understand their views, let me quote from my book *"Blood in the Streets: Concealed Carry and the OK Corral"*.

> "Sheep are born and bred for one purpose: to be killed and to have their parts processed into something useful by predators. They stand on the hill and go "Baa", as they're being slaughtered."

Now, first off, we have to understand that sheep disagree with the above statement. They believe they were born and bred to go to college, get a good job, make money, and raise a family who will then grow up themselves and perpetuate the flock. And of course they're right as well. We're both right, from our certain narrow points of view.

So why is there always such a huge disagreement between the unarmed public and those of us who carry pistols for self defense?

Enter the wolf. The wolf changes our perfect world into a world of danger. The wolf requires that some sheep grow fangs. The wolf changes everything.

As Lieutenant Colonel David Grossman has so astutely pointed out:

> "We know that the sheep live in denial, which is what makes them sheep. They do not want to believe that there is evil in the world."

I recall that as the concealed carry movement swept over our country, state by state like a cleansing wave, the sheep, almost without exception, were very quick to cry out their protests in one loud Baa! "No! No! Don't let them carry guns! We'll all be killed!"

History now tells us the vocal flock was wrong, and by and large, the sheep are beginning to tolerate the act of concealed carry for personal and family defense. So, if the flock accepts concealed carry (that is, people secretly carrying guns within the flock) then why are they so adamantly opposed to open carry? After all, guns are guns whether concealed or open. Right?

I think the answer lies in an email sent to me last week by a terrified sheep.

> "I was around during that terrible display when you had your little gun rally and I want you to know that if I ever see anyone in the grocery store with a gun I will call the police. I feel threatened when I see a gun and feel that it's a threat to my safety. I don't think that the 2nd amendment supersedes other people's right to not have to see a gun or be around one."

Now, it's interesting to note that I know this man, and I walk into his store quite often. He knows that I'm always armed and has never expressed fear. In fact, on one occasion he even asked me to teach him how to shoot. I saw him as a potential convert.

So what's the big difference? Why does he tolerate concealed carry, but not open carry? Once again Lt. Colonel David Grossman has the answer for us:

> "The sheep generally do not like the sheepdog. He looks a lot like the wolf. He has fangs and the capacity for violence. The difference, though, is that the sheepdog must not, cannot and will not ever harm the sheep. Any sheepdog who intentionally harms the lowliest little lamb will be punished and removed. Still, the sheepdog disturbs the

sheep. He is a constant reminder that there are wolves in the land."

Even though this man knows he is safe with me, he will call the police if he sees my gun. Is this irrational? Of course! Is he being consistent to his sheep-like personality? Absolutely!

He knows he's a sheep. He knows he's defenseless against anyone with a gun. I have a gun, therefore, in his way of thinking, I am a constant reminder that he is defenseless. His view is irrational, based solely on feelings, but also consistent with his sheep-like personality and his past views on concealed carry. Remember, it was this same sheep who fought hard to stifle concealed carry. He now accepts concealed carry simply because for many years we have walked among the flock and the sheep were not harmed. But this is where the sheep analogy breaks down; because people are not really sheep. They can think; they can learn; and they can change.

In my opinion, the sheep will one day grudgingly accept open carry just as they do concealed carry. But first they must be educated and desensitized to the sight of that awful, bad, mean "gun"! It will be a slow train coming, but it will come. Yesterday I was giving a radio interview and the talkshow host confided that when he was in Arizona, he saw many people walking around openly carrying pistols on their hips. At first it made him nervous and he didn't like it. But, after a few days of seeing it, he was no longer afraid. It was only then he noticed the terrified looks of other tourists who were seeing open carry for the very first time.

Yes, the sheep are restless. But the solution isn't to cater to the irrational fears of ignorance. The solution is the sensitive, responsible caring actions of sheepdogs who open carry. Whether you agree or disagree with open carry, the movement will succeed or fail based on its own actions. This is their battle to win or to lose.

But here is my bottom line: if they lead with wisdom and integrity, the sheep will follow. After all, that's what sheep do.

The Story Behind the Story

Many of my friends are opposed to open carry and at the very best unsure and hesitant about it. I think they feel this way primarily because it scares unarmed people. This article was written in an attempt to explain why so many people are against open carry, why it scares them, and even terrifies some. Some people have an irrational hatred and disdain for open carry. After research and experience, I think I understand why.

This article was my attempt at turning some irrational fear into sound, intellectual reason.

Twenty-two

Open Carry Debate Part 2 – The Armed Citizen's View

This installment of my commentary is a difficult one to write. Primarily because there are as many different views as there are armed citizens. Over the past week I've received dozens of emails from concealed carry holders, and their responses travel the full spectrum from: "Open Carry! Yes! Preach it! We have the right!" all the way over to "Open Carry will kill us all. It's just a bunch of macho jerks who want to flaunt their guns!"

Most of us, I suspect, are somewhere in between the two extremes.

The more typical response I'm getting is revealed by this email from a concealed carry holder near Detroit, Michigan. Here is an excerpt:

"I guess I fall into the "Sheepdog" category as you define it (the gray beard seems appropriate to that image, too).

I will support those who choose open carry, but cannot make that choice for myself. My objection boils down to one question: "Why advertise to the wolves?" I'd prefer that my armed status remain a surprise, especially if I need to make use of it."

He supports the right, but questions the tactical wisdom of it. Of course, open carry proponents argue that displaying a firearm is a useful deterrent. Unfortunately, I think that's a claim that is hard to prove except through personal experience. How can you possibly prove something didn't happen, that is, a crime did not occur because the bad guy was scared off? That leaves it open to opinion and speculation. In the end, each armed citizen will make his own decision as to how they carry.

It would be interesting to see the results of an objective survey with one answer allowed for the following question:

"Do you support the right to carry a pistol openly?"

1. Yes.

2. No.

3. Yes, but with reservations.

Based on my emails from the past week, I suspect that most people would vote for answer number 3.

Of course, not all of my email was positive or even neutral. I always seem to get a few people who strongly disagree with me or who even think I'm a foolish nut job.

I recall several months ago I received a scathing email from a reader who totally disagreed with my commentary. Here is a portion, with minor changes to respect the privacy of the author:

"I submit that an educated and "prominent" writer would

have found better literary devices to make the points,
unless, of course, the author is being deliberately condescending."

In retrospect, I was not being condescending, though I can understand why he may have misconstrued my purpose. I always have to be careful when I write, because people who don't know me personally are left to their own imaginations. Bottom line is, a commentary is provocative and opinionated by nature. More importantly, I touched the reader and made him think and feel, even though it took the form of lightning to a steel rod.

I used to be devastated by dissent, and it would cause me to slump into prolonged periods of not writing at all. When I shared my feelings with Ted Nugent (perhaps the biggest lightning rod in America) he gave me some very sage advice:

"Never fortify yourself against meaningful critique. There
is some wisdom there. Upgrade is limitless. Carry on!"

I took that advice to heart and it gave me the courage to write about such a controversial topic as open carry. I know going in that a few armed citizens will ridicule me for it, but that's the risk that one takes in this business. What a boring world it would be if everyone agreed with me. What could I possibly write about?

Finally, let's talk about the political types who are constantly analyzing, gauging, lifting their finger to the wind and check-ing the political pulses of citizens and legislators alike. Here is a valued excerpt from someone whom I trust both personally and politically:

"It's always a game of inches...arguing in any direction
to gain the inch is not bad strategy when you've lost the

battles to date (as the anti's have). Since no one will be able to effectively argue that 'open carry' helps in self-defense if you're armed anyway ('quicker draw' and 'intimidation of potential threats' will work against us...and the anti's know it), we're cooked. The conclusion will be that we're just a bunch of hotdogs looking to strap iron to our legs...a die-hard perception to this day. In other words, it will turn the heads of those 'average voters' that looked the other way and 'let us' win last time...right back at us. Flash steel and rub their noses in it and that will change... and Legislators--in the face of law enforcement struggling to keep a straight face--will prevail."

This, also is sage advice, coming from a person I respect, and someone in the position to gauge the political pulse. This is meaningful critique, and I will take Ted's advice and not fortify myself against it. I'll throw it into the mix with everything else before I come to a well-thought-out conclusion, as I hope you will as well.

The concern of many concealed carry holders is this: That all the gains we've fought so hard to achieve will be lost if people openly carry. The argument is that one idiot playing with his gun will accidentally shoot a kid and then it's Katie bar the door, because all manner of gun-control hell will be unleashed upon us.

That is a very real and valid fear. But hasn't that fear always been with us? Every time I read a news story about some idiot illegally brandishing a pistol or about a road rage situation, I feel that adrenaline surge deep in the pit of my stomach as I think to myself "Dear God, please don't let it be a concealed carry holder."

Because I know that the anti's would have a field day with it and make political hay.

However, I have to point out that by and large, that hasn't happened with concealed carry, and I suspect that neither will it happen with open carry. Now I could be wrong, but experience has taught me that honest, law-abiding gun owners are nothing to be feared, whether carrying openly or concealed.

But I fully understand the concerns and fears surrounding the sometimes controversial practice of open carry, because I share them. On the other hand, I wonder, how did America get to the point where the right to keep and bear arms would be considered controversial? That's the topic of a whole nuther commentary.

Keep those emails coming, even if you think I'm foolish. Sometimes, those make for the most interesting reading. Next week we delve into the final segment of this series as we explore the views of law enforcement and open carry.

The Story Behind the Story

I was surprised by the amount of negative criticism I took over my first open carry article. It was less than I thought it would be. Surprisingly, most concealed carriers, though they believe open carry is a bad idea, support the right of those who open carry. I found this encouraging. Personally, I believe we should universally support each other's right to keep and bear arms, whether that be assault rifles, dove hunting, concealed carry or open carry.

In short, a house divided cannot stand.

This is a biblical principle that was reaffirmed by President Lincoln in a speech he gave in Springfield, Illinois on June 16th 1858. He was speaking in terms of slavery, but the principle can be applied to gun ownership as well.

> "A house divided against itself cannot stand." I believe this government cannot endure permanently half slave and half free. I do not expect the Union to be dissolved -- I do not expect the house to fall -- but I do expect it will cease to be divided. It will become all one thing, or all the other."

The same is true with the right to keep and bear arms. If gun owners divide against themselves, then our house will fall. We must stand, unite, and support all brands of the Second Amendment, regardless of the form we prefer.

Twenty-three

Open Carry Debate Part 3 – A Cop's Eye View

I love my family. I have a 2-year old little boy and he's cuter than the dickens. I have 4 other kids whom I love and, of course, my wife, Sara, she's the best. I would willingly, without hesitation, give my life to protect any of them from harm. Every police officer I know feels the same way about their own family. They are husbands and wives, mothers and fathers, and they love their families every bit as much as we civilians love ours.

Despite that great love we have in common, I'm beginning to notice a bit of animosity between armed civilians and law enforcement. Some armed citizens resent the way a few rogue police officers view them with suspicion. Conversely, a few police officers resent the way civilians are allowed to openly carry firearms. In my opinion, there is room for improvement on both sides.

Being a Second Amendment activist and a firearms instructor, I've had occasion to become friends with quite a few officers.

I am happy to report that almost all of them supported our right to keep and bear arms. But my personal experience is limited and I wanted to draw on a larger cross section for this commentary, so I did some research. I registered on a police internet talk forum. I went to their "Ask a Cop" section and here is how they answered my questions:

1. What do you think when you see a civilian carrying openly?

• "I think it's someone who is trying to make a political point in a very irresponsible way."

• "It seems to me that open carry is a fast way to an open casket. As has been stated when the shooting starts, the one with the visible weapon is the first target. As an officer, if I'm in a bad situation."

2. Do you see him as a threat? Do you assume certain things?

• "I don't necessarily see a person carrying openly as any more of a threat than a person carrying concealed. A lot of people carry concealed with no problems."

3. Does open carry make your job more difficult?

• "The biggest problem would be that many citizens will call 911 when they see the gun being carried out in the open. Now, as an Officer, I have to at least contact the person with the gun to see what's up. That's not a problem if the man with the gun acts reasonably and is willing to understand that I need to do my job and do it safely."

• "I'm sure that the pretext stop on someone carrying just to check if the person is legal, is going to be a pain in the rear, because you know that the bad guys will start to carry openly also."

- "There are places where such open carry may be 'socially appropriate' but, in today's urban-based society, these are few and far. An 'open carry' in parts of Alaska, Arizona, Idaho or Texas will be of far less concern than in Oakland, Los Angeles, downtown Dallas, or Miami ... I feel much the same way about someone openly carrying a large knife, a ball bat, a Samurai sword, an axe or a chain saw; does the item, locale and behavior fit the situation?"

As you can see, there are as many different opinions as there are cops, so what exactly is the "Cop's-Eye View" on open carry? A few days ago I was golfing with my County Sheriff, so during our 4 hours on the course, I picked his brain for a more balanced and realistic view. In his opinion it all depends on the jurisdiction – that is, the more rural the setting, the more acceptable open carry. People in the country grow up using guns, so they are not afraid of them, whereas, people in the city associate guns with crime. I tend to agree with the Sheriff's analysis.

Does that mean we should never carry in cities? No, of course not. It just means that you might be stopped by police officers if you do. Let's face it, law enforcement is not the easiest job in the world. Most of a cop's clientele are the lowest of the low, the bottom feeders of society. A police officer can quickly become distrusting and suspicious. I don't blame him. I probably would too.

On the other hand, law enforcement isn't supposed to be easy. It has always been difficult and it always will be. Nothing will ever change that short of a total loss of freedom. They are the messengers, enforcing laws which, in some cases, shouldn't even exist. Because of this, Police will usually see people at their worst.

Nonetheless, there are a few cops who just don't understand the concept of civil liberty. I wish I didn't have to mention them, but I'd be derelict if I didn't. Just a month ago, Chris Fetters was arrested in the city of Grand Haven for obeying the law. Yes, you heard me right. He was arrested for obeying the law. He was openly carrying within the city limits. According to Chris, two officers came up behind him, each grabbed an arm and they threw him against a wall pinning him there while disarming him. To his credit, Chris didn't resist. They took him to be interrogated, detaining him for an hour. He tried to explain that open carry was legal, but the officers insisted he was in violation of a city ordinance. They confiscated his Glock and wouldn't listen to him. Chris will be in court this week defending his freedom in every sense of the word.

Ironically, it was the Grand Haven Police Department who was in violation of the law and not Chris Fetters. The ordinance they cited him with is unenforceable since it violates the Michigan Firearms Preemption Law. Chris now has a lawyer. I'll keep you posted on that one.

Like I said, there is room for improvement on both sides.

People who want to open carry, even though it is undeniably legal in 44 states, must do so with the understanding that a few police officers will arrest them. They must be patient; they must be kind; and they must be compliant and cooperative as they're being hauled away in handcuffs. Let's face it, if you want to be point man on open carry, or any other controversial political movement, you're going to pay a price. Ask Rosa Parks – she'll tell you.

Police officers need to educate themselves and accept the fact that their jobs are difficult. Yes, I understand why open carry makes it tough for you, and while I sympathize with you, I'm not about to give up my right to keep and bear arms to make your job easier.

However, I will do my best to shorten your discomfort by helping to educate the numb nuts who keep dialing 911 because they see someone obeying the law. They are the real problem. It's not the open carriers and it's not the police. It's the gutless, ignorant sheep who insist on their unconstitutional right to "feel" safe. In my opinion, the best way to feel safe, is to be safe! Take an NRA pistol course, get some marksmanship instruction, then buy a pistol and take responsibility for your own safety.

In my way of thinking, it's time the three sides: police, open carriers, and sheep, all got together. Stop the ignorance and fear. Start seeing one another as humans and not as political pawns. After all, when the rubber meets the road, we're just mothers and fathers, husbands and wives – we're just people who want to live through the day and come home safely to the families we love.

The Story Behind the Story

This was probably the toughest installment of the series for me to write. I felt like I was walking on the apex of a very sharp knife and if I fell to one side or the other, I'd be cut to shreds.

On the one hand, some armed citizens have been denied their civil rights by a few police officers. On the other hand, police officers sometimes get shot at while trying to defend us. I had to present both sides fairly and accurately without favoring one or the other. To do so would be wrong and would invite criticism by one party or both.

After I was done writing, it occurred to me that neither the police nor the person open carrying is the real problem. The person who starts all the trouble is the irrational, terrified sheep who picks up the phone and dials 911.

Perhaps the best way to go forward is to deny these sheep the right to keep and bear cell phones? Okay, yes, I'm kidding, but the thought had occurred to me.

Twenty-four

A Summary of the Open Carry Debate – The Pros and the Cons

Those of you who subscribe to the MCRGO Enewsletter, know that I just finished a 3-part series on the Open Carry Debate. Those of you who don't subscribe, may want to log on to www.mcrgo.org and take care of that. There's lots of good information in there and it comes out every Monday morning. Along with articles written by myself and others, you'll find a weekly *Ask the Lawyer* section written by our own Steve Dulan, Attorney and MCRGO Board member. It's top-notch and you should check it out.

For those who haven't read the series, let me bring you up to speed. Historically, I have been adamantly opposed to open carry for the following reasons:

1. There is no tactical advantage.
2. It scares people.

A few months ago, through a series of circumstances, I took

it upon myself to organize an open carry march in the city of Hastings, Michigan, where close to 50 people came and marched through town openly carrying their holstered firearms. The goals of the march were as follows:

1. To educate the public, the media and law enforcement that open carry was both legal and constitutional.

2. To demonstrate that gun owners need not be feared by the general population.

For years I've been practicing concealed carry, but have always been afraid that someone would see my firearm and call the police. (Actually, this has happened to me as well as to many others.) And then it occurred to me:

Why am I more afraid of law enforcement than I am of a brutal criminal? I'm trained and able to handle bad guys; they try to kill me and I defend myself. But it's not so cut and dried with police officers. If they believe you are breaking the law, even when you're not, they will arrest you, cite you, and then you'll have to spend tens of thousands of dollars defending yourself in court. There is justice in America – as much as you can afford to buy.

That question on law enforcement still bothers me, and I've been thinking about it for a long time. What happens if a police officer no longer respects the law? What happens if a police officer sworn to uphold our civil rights, decides to pick and choose which ones to defend and which ones to deny?

I don't like asking these questions, primarily because of its scary, far-reaching ramifications, and secondarily because I'll be misconstrued as anti-police, which is not true at all. But I can't deny that there are a few rogue police officers out there who abuse their power by denying us the right to keep and bear arms. We saw it in the concealed carry debate, and now we're seeing it again with open carry. Part 3 of my series dealt with law enforcement and open carry, so I won't go into it in detail again. Suffice it to say that the vast majority of police officers support your right to keep and bear arms. However, you do have to be prepared to be arrested if you open carry in some jurisdictions in many states. At least for now, it's a fact of life.

And that begs another question: "What good is a right if you're not allowed to exercise it? In fact, if you're arrested when you open carry, then are you really free to do it?

But I digress, so let's get back on track again. At the open carry march I held in Hastings, it was, in every sense, a smashing success and one of the best times I've ever had. During that event, a strange and unexpected thing happened to me. I was no longer nervous about being arrested. In fact, I was downright happy, gleeful even. It felt good to no longer have to hide my pistol behind a shirt. At that moment, while walking down main street with all eyes watching, I felt more like a free man than at any other point in my life.

And now, I find myself in a dilemma. I want to open carry for several reasons. When I practice open carry, I feel more like a citizen, and less like a subject. Also, I can wear anything I want without the hassle of covering up that piece of iron.

Those of you who know me, realize that I'm not one to passively accept something that's bothering me. So for the past few months, I've been researching the open carry debate and coming to some conclusions of my own. Let me share my findings with you, and then you can form your own opinions.

First, what are the down sides to open carry? Second, are these down sides logical and valid?

1. You might be arrested.

2. You might be disarmed by criminals who see your pistol.

3. You might scare the sheep.

Fear of arrest is both logical and valid. I don't believe you should be arrested for open carry, just as you shouldn't be arrested for any other legal act. But realities being as they are, you still might be arrested in many urban jurisdictions for open carry. Let's face it, police officers have over 22,000 gun laws to enforce, so it's no wonder they get it wrong sometimes. Case in point, I once asked police officers if I am required to carry my pistol safety inspection certificate with me while carrying my firearm. I asked 5 different cops , therefore, I got five different and conflicting answers. (I should note that the same thing happens with lawyers, pistol instructors, and pastors. Opinions vary, but the law must remain constant.)

As for being disarmed by criminals who see your pistol? Well, that just doesn't happen. How can I say that? Because I asked 59 different people on the www.opencarry.org website who routinely open carry in varying urban and rural areas. Of the 59 open carriers, only 3 of them had been disarmed. (It's noteworthy to say that all 3 were disarmed by police officers, and not by criminals.) Of all the open carriers I've spoken with, almost all of them practice heightened awareness and some form of pistol retention. In fact, most open carriers are also CPL holders, whom we already know to be responsible and safe firearm owners.

That brings us to number 3. You might scare the sheep. This is a very valid and logical concern. And it's undoubtedly true, to a certain degree. In order to put this to the test, I started carrying openly in low-risk situations about 2 months ago. (By low-risk, I mean rural, pro-gun communities, with low-crime rates.) I was astounded at what happened. Out of the hundreds of people who passed me by, only one noticed that I was carrying a pistol. He asked me if I was a police officer. I said no and he just said "Oh, I thought you were." I found this rather disappointing and anticlimactic. Here I was expecting all kinds of fireworks, hand-cuffs, arrest, interrogation with bright lights and dripping water, etc., and all I got were the blank looks of people hurrying about, minding their own business.

My gun just didn't phase these country folk.

While writing part 2 of my series I was forced to find out what CPL holders thought of open carry. To that end, I asked good old "WebJim" to put the following poll on www.mcrgo.org:

"Do you support the right to carry a pistol openly?"

1. Yes.

2. No.

3. Yes, but with reservations.

Once again, I was amazed at the results of the 445 CPL holders who responded.

Yes – 75%

No – 5%

Yes, but with reservations – 20%

Now, in all fairness, many of those voting yes admitted that they chose not to open carry for fear of legal and political repercussions, but it was encouraging to learn that they see the Second Amendment as an all-encompassing right to keep and bear arms, whether open or concealed.

Which brings me to my own personal opinion. I vote wholeheartedly "yes" to that question. However, I must admit that I still only open carry in rural settings. Primarily because, I just don't want the trauma of arrest. I don't have time for it. How would I get anything done? Besides, my wife would get mad at me for sitting in jail while she sits home alone watching the kids.

But I do like the way the Michigan branch of the www.opencarry.org forum has been handling open carry events.

They set up picnics all across the state in public parks where open carriers can meet and socialize with little fear of arrest. Just this past summer they've held picnics in Grand Rapids, Warren, and Burton. All three events got lots of media and law enforcement coverage. Everyone was waiting for something bad to happen, but nothing did. In fact, law enforcement and city officials were notified ahead of time to ensure that things went smoothly.

It was just a bunch of American families getting together, eating good food, and making friends. It sounds like a good time to me, and I plan on attending some of these picnics. It's a safe venue, where people can come and learn, and try on open carry for size. No longer do you have to drive to some far-off Western state to get the experience of open carry. You can safely do it right here in Michigan.

In closing, open carry is not for everyone, but it might be for you. Try it out and see. But first, take the time to get pistol-retention training, carry a pistol-retention holster, and always remain at a state of heightened awareness. It's a right that you can't take lightly.

The Story Behind the Story

This was my fifth and final article on open carry. All in all it was a good experience for me and I learned a lot and made many good friends throughout the RKBA society. It has been several months since my open carry march in Hastings, but I still open carry once in a while just for grins.

But I have to admit that while it was fun, I still prefer concealed carry most of the time. I think that has more to do with my personality than anything else. It's not a tactical concern or fear about arrest, it's just that I don't like to be noticed. I prefer to keep a low profile, to go about my business without people looking at me or asking me questions. That's probably the writer part of me. Most of us artist/author types are a bit introverted to begin with and would rather hole up in a cave with a laptop somewhere than socialize. My wife will probably never like that part of me.

I still go on the opencarry.org website sometimes to see what's going on, and I will go to some of their picnics next Spring when it warms up.

The sad thing about the whole open carry debate, is the emotional division that pervades it. It reminds me of the hunting community. I've seen it happen so often and the anti's just love it when we argue with each other. Here are some examples:

Hunting with dogs is bad.

Hunting Mourning Doves is bad.

Bowhunting with a modern compound bow really isn't bow hunting.

Hunting with a crossbow is bad.

Hunting over bait is not sporting and not really hunting.

I suppose in my opinion, we should tolerate each other as much as we can. In fact, I'll go even further than that. Not only should we tolerate each other's preferences, we should mutually support them.

The practical application would sound like this:

"I prefer not to hunt Mourning Doves, but you go ahead so long as it's legal."

"I prefer the challenge of a wooden longbow, but you shoot any bow you like."

"Crossbows? You go ahead, so long as it's legal in that state. Same thing for hunting over bait."

Sometimes we get so dogmatic and intolerant as sportsmen and gun owners that we tend to cannibalize our own teammates. We need to get away from that. Let's just live and let live.

Twenty-five

Klondike Bars and Ice-Cold Frappuccino

Many things in this world are worth living for. Some things in life are worth fighting for. Some are even worth dying for. But have you ever asked this question: what things in life – are worth killing for? It's a basic question, one that everyone should know the answer to, but I just don't hear many people asking it. However, for those of us who carry guns, the question hits closer to home.

I already know what's worth fighting for: lower taxes, my little brother and sister when we were kids, a Klondike bar and an ice-cold Frappuccino, and every four years I fight for my presidential candidate of choice. But would I die for these things? I think not. I hate taxes, but I wouldn't die for a tax cut. My siblings when we were young? I fought for them all the time. Nobody picks on my little brothers and sisters except me, but I never fought to the death. We were just kids and death was the farthest thing from our minds. What would I do for a Klondike bar? Well, I love a good Klondike bar as much as the next guy, and I've got an ice-cold Frappaccino beside me even as I type. But I wouldn't clear leather for either. And that leaves us with my presidential candidate. Let's just say I wouldn't have made a very good Secret Service Agent.

But on the flip side, the moment I saw my first child I knew I would die for him. No one touches my kids! No one touches my wife! And as long as we're at it, you'd best leave my aging mother alone too! In short, my family is off limits to bad guys. You hurt my family, and you'll have to answer to me. I'm simple that way.

I would die for my country, though, as a United States Marine, many years ago, I was thankful for peacetime.

I would die for God. Wasn't it Jim Elliot, the South American missionary, who once said and later gave his life: "He is no fool who gives up what he cannot keep to gain that which he cannot lose."

God – Family – Country. I would fight for all three. I would die for all three. I would live for all three. But what would I kill for? That's another matter altogether.

A few days ago I was speaking at a church to a local MOPS group. MOPS stands for Mothers of Preschoolers. So I was standing up in front of 25 soccer moms bouncing babies and toddlers on their laps, and I remember thinking "Here I am an NRA Pistol Instructor, the author of several books including one called "*Blood in the Streets*". Normally I talk about guns, bullets, personal protection, you know, the basics of life. But I just had a feeling that most of them wouldn't relate to that.

And then I was reminded of another mother of a preschooler

that I had taught many years ago in a concealed carry class. At first I couldn't relate to her, but then we turned out to have more in common than I'd thought. The story goes like this.

I was teaching a husband and wife in a private lesson on their farm in southwest Michigan. We were on the range behind their barn, shooting at targets up against an embankment.

The woman was shooting a nice, 9mm Glock, and she honestly could not hit the broad side of a barn from the inside. I tried everything I knew to get her on target, but it was no use. I couldn't find the problem. Her husband told me she was a good shot, and that she usually shot better than he did, so he didn't understand the problem either. I questioned her some more, and she finally threw up her hands in frustration and said, "I don't even know why I'm doing this! I could never shoot a real person anyways. My husband made me take this class!"

At her remark, a light went off in my head, and I interjected. "What if someone was trying to kill you? Could you shoot someone then?"

She said, "No! I couldn't kill someone to save my own life. I'd just go ahead and die!" I thought that was rather odd, but I could tell she was sincere, so I thought about it a second. Even though most people have an aversion to killing another human, I personally believe that there are very few people on this planet who would rather die than protect themselves. Almost everyone has a point where they will cross the line and take a life.

Earlier in the day, this couple had introduced me to their baby girl, so I said,

"How old is your daughter?"

"Nine months."

"Okay, let's use a little training technique called visualization."

She nodded her head impatiently.

"Okay, here's the scenario: You're at the gas station filling your tank. A man drives up and parks next to your car. He gets out, walks over, reaches through the open window of your car, removes your daughter from her car seat and puts her in his own vehicle. He then starts to get inside to drive away."

There was a horrified look on the young mother's face.

"At that moment in time, could you take another human life?"

She said, "I would kill that son of a bitch!"

I said, "Okay then, that target down there is that man who is stealing your daughter. Fire away."

She never missed the target again.

So there I was, looking out over 25 mothers of preschoolers, and then I knew what to talk about. I knew what we had in common: our children – our spouses – our families.

I think it's that way with a lot of people. At first glance we just don't seem to have anything in common, but that is rarely true. I know rich people, poor people, rednecks, sophisticated people, conservatives, liberals and I'm friends with them all. I think sometimes us pro-gunners alienate ourselves unnecessarily. Some of us on occasion can get a bit uppity and self righteous thinking that we have the corner on truth. Then we start looking down on people different than us. But when the rubber meets the road, when the cows come home, when the chickens come home to roost – we're all basically the same.

We love our kids. We love our wives. We love God. We love our country.

It's just the details that wrap us around the axle.

So back to my original question: What would I kill for? I'd kill to maintain liberty. I'd definitely kill to protect my family. I'd even kill for God, though I doubt He'd ever ask me too.

But the rest of you have to figure it out for yourselves. And the time to do it is now. Once someone sticks a gun in your face, it's too late. Deciding when to kill is not a fun thing; it's down-right distasteful, but CPL holders have to do it. So if you're car-rying a gun and haven't answered that question, best do so now while you still can.

The Story Behind the Story

When teaching my basic concealed carry classes, I sometimes tell my students this:

"You're in the local gas station, in the back by the cooler, get-ting a Mountain Dew. You look over and see a man pointing a revolver at the clerk and demanding money. You are armed with a pistol and a cell phone. Please tell me in detail exactly what you would do."

Then I go around the room and I have three people give me their best answer. I make sure they all know that there is no right or wrong answer, but I remind them that people will live or die based on their decision.

I have found that men are more likely to intervene than

women, and that military veterans almost always intervene.

After they give their answer, I go over in detail what my response would be and I point out that not everyone has equal abilities, and that not everyone can and should intervene.

It's interesting to note that those who choose not to intervene sometimes judge the interventionist as brutal and cold-blooded. Conversely, the interventionist sometimes sees those not using deadly force as cowardly or lacking compassion for their fellow man.

In reality, there is only one answer, and that is the one you choose. In the end, you will live or die based on the decision that you make. It's not right; it's not wrong; it just "is".

The only wrong thing is not taking the time and effort to figure it out before strapping on your firearm. What would you live for? What would you die for? What would you kill for? All basic questions in life. It's amazing how many people never take the time to think about it.

Take the time, now, while you still can. Be prepared. Stay alive.

Twenty-six

The Thin Veneer of Civilization

The threat of global terrorism, Iran developing nuclear weapons, 60+ killed by homicide bomber in Islamabad, multiple hurricanes hitting Texas, gas at over 4 dollars a gallon, and to top it all off, many say the American economy (that's us) is on the verge of total meltdown.

And my wife wonders why I have to go hunting so much.

Sometimes I just have to get away from the television, from the internet, from the radio, and from every other confounded form of electrical technology known to man.

So a few days ago, when Michigan's early doe season opened up, I drug my disillusioned, stressed-out carcass into the woods and sat within sight of a cornfield, waiting for the first unsuspecting doe to pop her unlucky head out of the corn. It's not that I like to kill things, because I really don't. The final kill of the hunt has always been a bit anticlimactic for me, even a little reverent and humbling. Sure, I love the challenge of the hunt, and, to be certain, I love to provide meat for the table, but, without a doubt, most of all, I just need to get away.

Reminds me of that song from the old sitcom "*Cheers*" with Sam and Woody and Norm. Except it's the antithesis of all that. Instead of wanting to go where everybody knows my name, I want to go where no one knows my name, where I can just climb a tree and melt into the oneness of the woods. I need that sometimes.

It was a hot day for fall, with not much of a breeze, but, every once in a while, the wind would kick up and the corn leaves would brush up against each other. I knew that even while I sat calmly in my tree stand, that a thousand miles away Wall Street was careening towards destruction and doom, taking the rest of the civilized world with it. But I just didn't care. Sometimes, in order to survive, you have to rise above the uncontrollable things and latch on to something more universal and something greater than ourselves. I suppose a body could go crazy if he never rose above the fray, climbed a tree and shrugged it all off.

Time in the woods is also time to reflect, to find your center, to re-evaluate who you are and where you want to go. I did that as I watched the sun go down over the cornfield. I realized that I'd been letting others control my life, that I'd gotten too busy, and that I needed to seize the day and slow my life down again.

After a few hours of reflection and relaxation, the tightness in my chest, and the knots in my stomach began to loosen up and go away. An hour before sunset, I saw the top of a cornstalk wiggling back and forth. I smiled. It was showtime.

The deer ate inside the corn for a half hour before I saw her. Finally, when she stepped out of the last row of corn, I surmised that she was a healthy, average-sized doe with my family's name written all over her. She was alert and I could tell she sensed something was wrong by the way she stomped her foot. I've always been amazed by these animals and their senses and survival instincts. I waited until her head turned away before raising my Remington 870, putting the crosshairs right behind the shoulder about halfway up her body. She was a beautiful animal, and, for a moment, I considered letting her go. That moment of power and truth is always interesting for me. Because, at that moment, I hold the power of life and death in my hands; it's totally up to me whether that deer lives or dies. Sometimes, I lower my gun and just watch until they walk away.

This time, I released the safety, eased back on the trigger and felt the gun recoil against my shoulder. The doe jumped off to her left and started on her last run through the corn. My heart-rate was up a little, but not like it was when I was younger. I settled back down on the seat of my Lone Wolf tree stand and closed my eyes. The sun was almost down and the air had a bit of chill to it. I heard a squirrel off in the distance. Beside me, 20 feet up, I glanced over at a woodpecker eating bugs off the side of a dead tree. I was a world away from cataclysm on Wall Street, from homicide bombers in Pakistan, and from muggers in Detroit and downtown Chicago.

When I'm out in the woods, it's hard to fathom that the world of electricity and the world of deer hunting are interconnected. How can two so diametrically different lifestyles exist on the same planet.

But they do. And they will. Forever.

I was teaching a class of 25 concealed carry students yesterday, and I digressed a bit when I told them: "There is but a thin veneer of civilization that holds our society together. That veneer is artificial. It's not real. And it's very fragile. The only thing that holds it in place is accountability and the rule of law. And when a man can murder someone, spend 5 years in jail, then get out to murder again, then the veneer gets even thinner. When the rule of law breaks down, there is no accountability in life. And when God is removed from the equation, there is no accountability after death. What does that leave us? The law of the jungle, where only the strongest survive."

By the time you read this commentary, Wall Street will be opening, and Congress will be deciding the fate of our economy. I have very little faith in either entity. I just don't trust greedy businessmen or power-hungry politicians.

After dark, I got down out of my treestand, unpacked my flashlight and took up the bloodtrail. It was generous and wide. Helen Keller could have followed this bloodtrail. Five minutes later I gutted her out and drug her back to the edge of the corn. I sat down to rest and looked up at the stars. They were beautiful. And I thought to myself. "This is what I trust, God and my Model 870."

Even if the market opens tomorrow and plummets to zero, I won't be shaken, because I never trusted it. Government, politics, Wall Street – it's just veneer - just something artificial that makes us humans look better than we really are. I suspect that when the veneer is stripped away, a lot more of us will be out here in the woods unwinding, reconnecting with God, finally figuring out what is important and what is not.

The Story Behind the Story

I wrote that article two months ago. Since then, two more deer have fallen in my wake: one yearling and one small buck with lots of meat on them. I don't hunt for trophies. I just hunt to untie the knots and to fill the freezer. I spent all of today cutting and grinding the deer I shot with my bow two days ago. I like doing it myself. It's hard work, but it draws me closer to the earth, closer to the real stuff and farther from the thin veneer of civilization, that artificial thing, that fake and manmade stuff that can never last.

This coming Saturday is the gun-deer opener here in Michigan as well as in other states across the country. I'll be out there, freezing my butt off, becoming one with nature, playing the predator, shooting the first unlucky deer to stumble across my path. I used to hunt all season for big antlers, but I no longer have the time or enthusiasm for it. Sure, I'll shoot a big buck if he asks me to. But I'll be just as happy with a nice, fat doe. More importantly, I just want to hear the wind in the trees and feel the absence of electricity.

Sometimes I just want to go where no one knows my name.

Twenty-Seven

In Closing

Well, I don't know about you, but I've really enjoyed our time together and I hope to see you again soon. I'll keep writing, telling you who I am and giving you my two cents worth. Hopefully I won't offend you, but, who knows, I just might. It's not my goal though.

I'd like to leave you with a few thoughts and admonitions.

First, love God and obey his commandments. If you can't love Him, then at least obey Him and respect His position. It's wise advice. Especially since he's bigger than we are. (He's God - I'm not.)

Second, love your family. Treat your spouse with respect and courtesy. Always put your partner first. Never go to bed mad at each other and don't be afraid to compromise or even give in once in a while. It can't hurt. Your kids should tow the line, but always treat them with dignity and never provoke them to anger without just cause. That's from the good book too, so I know I'm right on that one.

Last, but certainly not least, honor your country. America is still the greatest nation on this planet and she is worthy your service and praise. Where else on earth can you be so free? Where else are you so fully guaranteed your right to keep and bear arms? (Even if the government can be a bit cranky about it at times.)

One thing is for certain, America is better because of the right to keep and bear arms. It lets us protect our families; it keeps us safe at night; it even gives us the means to rebel against a tyrannical government should they get too far out of line. But even in this, a firearm is a tool of last resort.

Thanks for being my Second Amendment ally. Keep fighting for upgrade. Never give in to those who would shackle your freedom. I leave you with the famous words of Mark Twain:

> "In the beginning of a change, the patriot is a scarce man, brave and hated and scorned. When his cause succeeds the timid join him, for then it costs nothing to be a patriot."

Thanks for coming and don't be scarce. You can all sit by my fire anytime.

God bless you and your family.

Skip Coryell
The Author
www.skipcoryell.com
www.mwtac.com
skipcoryell@hotmail.com

Skip Coryell now lives with his wife and children in Michigan. He works full time as a professional writer, and *"RKBA: Defending the Right to Keep and Bear Arms"* is his sixth published book. He is an avid hunter and sportsman who loves the outdoors. Skip is also a Marine Corps veteran, a graduate of Cornerstone University, and the Chief Pistol Instructor for Ted Nugent United Sportsmen of Michigan. Skip is the former Michigan State Director for Ted Nugent's organization. He has also served on the Board of Directors for Michigan Sportsmen against Hunger as well as Iowa Carry Inc. He is a Certified NRA Pistol Instructor and Range Safety Officer, teaching the Personal Protection in the Home Course for those wishing to obtain their Concealed Pistol Permits (www.mwtac.com). He also teaches Advanced Concealed Carry Classes for the more seasoned shooter. Skip is the President of White Feather Press and the co-owner of Midwest Tactical Training.

For more details on Skip Coryell, or to contact him personally, go to his website at www.skipcoryell.com (email: skip@whitefeatherpress.com).

God who gave us life gave us liberty. And can
the liberties of a nation be thought secure
when we have removed their only firm basis,
a conviction in the minds of the people that
these liberties are a gift from God? ... Indeed I
tremble for my country when I reflect that God is
just, and that His justice cannot sleep forever.
— Thomas Jefferson —

Suggested Resources

Below is my list of books, websites, and schools, where you can learn more information related to protecting your family and the Right to Keep and Bear Arms.

Books:

Author, Massad Ayoob

"In the gravest extreme "

"Gun-proof your children "

"The truth about self-protection "

"Stressfire—gunfighting tactics for police"

Author, Ted Nugent

"God, Guns, and Rock-n-roll"

"Ted, White and Blue"

Author, Lt. Col. David Grossman

"Stop Teaching Our Kids to Kill: A Call to Action Against TV, Movie and Video Game Violence"

"On Killing: The Psychological Cost of Learning to Kill in War and Society"

Author, Jim Cirillo

"Guns, Bullets, and Gunfights: Lessons and Tales from a Modern-Day Gunfighter"

Author, Jeff Cooper

"Principles of Self Defense"

Author, Clayton Cramer

"Firing Back"

"Concealed Weapon Laws of the Early Republic: Dueling, Southern Violence, and Moral Reform"

Author, Robert Dykstra

"The Cattle Towns"

Author, Daniel and Carol Bambery

"A Common Sense Guide to Michigan Gun Laws"

Author, Skip Coryell

"RKBA: Defending the Right to Keep and Bear Arms"

"Blood in the Streets: Concealed Carry and the OK Corral"

"Laughter and Tears: Living both Sides of Life"

"We Hold These Truths"

"Bond of Unseen Blood"

"Church and State"

Author, Mark Gabriel, PH.D.

"Islam and Terrorism"

"Islam and the Jews"

Author, Steven Emerson

"American Jihad: The Terrorists Living Among Us"

Author, Wayne LaPierre

"The Global War on Your Guns"

Advanced Firearms Training:

Midwest Training Group (Bob Houzenga) Iowa
www.midwesttraininggroup.net

(For Idaho school, call Andy Kemp at 630-335-6661)

Lethal Force Institute (Massad Ayoob) Held throughout the United States - go to www.ayoob.com for details

American Small Arms Academy (Chuck Taylor) Arizona
www.chucktaylorasaa.com

Defense Training International (John Farnam) Colorado
www.defense-training.com

Firearms Academy of Seattle, Washington
www.firearmsacademy.com
Front Sight Firearms Training Institute, Nevada
www.frontsight.com
Thunder Ranch (Clint Smith) Oregon
www.thunderranchinc.com
Websites:

www.killology.com

www.ayoob.com

www.mcrgo.org

www.nra.org

www.tednugent.com

www.mwtac.com

www.jpfo.org

www.gunowners.org

www.saf.org

www.iowacarry.org

www.wisconsinconcealedcarry.com

www.missouricarry.com

www.ccrkba.org

www.ohioccw.org

www.usconcealedcarry.com

www.illinoiscarry.com

www.concealedcampus.org

www.isra.org

Coming in March of 2009!

"*Stalking Natalie*"

The all-new suspense thriller by Skip Coryell will be available on March 1st 2009.

The city had been gripped in terror for months as it was stalked by a vicious and deadly serial killer. Natalie Katrell, a lonely, single mom, was just trying to make it on her own and provide for her daughter when she was savagely attacked and hospitalized. Determined to fight back, she meets up with retired police officer and pistol instructor Sam Colton who agrees to teach her the skills she'll need to protect herself and her young daughter should the killer return.

"But neither Natalie nor Amethyst could see the man watching them. He always stayed off in the shadows, hidden around corners, or gazing from behind the innocent pages of a paperback book. Sometimes he sipped tea while at other times he nursed a vanilla latte with a double shot of espresso. But always, without fail, he watched Natalie and her daughter. He was obsessed and Natalie was his next *chosen* one."

Order your copy online at www.whitefeatherpress.com and find out how Natalie fights back!

www.ingramcontent.com/pod-product-compliance
Lightning Source LLC
Chambersburg PA
CBHW072144270326
41931CB00010B/1881